Gerda von Bülow
Treasures of Thrace

Photographs by
Wolfgang G. Schröter

St. Martin's Press
New York

We would like to express our deep appreciation to the National Cultural Committee of Bulgaria for its assistance with the photographic material and for granting us permission to publish the plates.

Translated from the German by Peter Underwood

Design and drawings by Sonja Wunderlich

Library of Congress Catalog Card Number: 85-43358
ISBN 0-312-81649-9

First Published in the German Democratic Republic by Edition Leipzig

First U.S. Edition

10 9 8 7 6 5 4 3 2 1

Contents

1 Map of the areas populated by Thracian tribes on the Balkan peninsula

Historical Background

The Balkan peninsula was always an important intersection of major communication routes between Asia and Europe. In the course of the millennia, it witnessed continual migratory waves. Emanating from the Asiatic steppes or from a south-easterly direction, these routes skirted both the northern and southern coasts of the Black Sea before meeting at the lower Danube, which they then followed to central and western Europe. A third line of communication led from the Mediterranean via Greece towards the north-east. The Balkan peninsula itself possesses many natural assets: a mild climate, albeit not as warm as that of Greece, and fertile plains nestling between protective wooded mountains, which in addition are connected with the open sea by a labyrinth of rivers (pl. **1**).

All these factors provided favorable conditions for the relatively early settlement of the areas between the lowlands along the lower Danube, bounded in the north by the Carpathians, and the Aegean coast. In the Neolithic period (between the 6th and the 4th millennium B.C.) an advanced civilization developed here, which was in close touch with the cultures that had emerged in Asia Minor. Via these latter it also came into contact with the early advanced civilizations that were forming in western Asia. These diverse influences helped to promote the economic and cultural development of the Balkan peninsula which, however, acquired a character of its own because of its particular conditions.

The Neolithic Age was marked by the beginning of a sedentary way of life, which in turn was connected with the start of systematic attempts to develop farming. On the Balkan peninsula, particularly in the extremely fertile areas lying in the south and south-east of what is to-day Bulgaria, there are thus numerous ancient farming settlements. More than 400 such sites, which in the course of time have developed into hills—or tells—as a result of the accumulation of deposits of debris, are known to exist in Bulgaria alone. Often they lie in river valleys at the bases of mountain ranges. The dwellings were normally rectangular or square in shape and made of wood and mud with a roof of wood or straw. The earliest houses consisted of a single room with a hearth at the back. In the later Neolithic period a working room was added in which, in a number of excavations, stone mortars and hand mills for grinding grain have been found.

The sedentary life and the beginning of production based on the division of labor led to the development of a system of storage. Initially the grain, mostly wheat and barley, was stored in large vessels of wicker covered with clay, but gradually the systematic production of clay vessels developed and by the Neolithic period had already reached a high technical and artistic level. Ceramic articles for everyday use were characterized by a multiplicity of forms and a wide range of decoration (pl. **2**).

Owing to the lack of written records the names of the races which were the bearers of this early culture on the Balkan peninsula have been lost. However, archaeological finds indicate a direct line of development right up to the Thracian civilization of the late Bronze Age (second half of the 2nd millennium B.C.), so that the Thracians at least had some roots going back as far as the Neolithic culture on the Balkan peninsula. In later times numerous waves of migration, again stemming from the east and south-east, also played an important part in the formation of the Thracian nation as we understand it in the 1st millennium B.C. It was a long and complex ethnogenetic process in the course of which the continual influx of foreign tribes provided fresh impulses for the social and cultural development of the native elements, which slowly merged with the new arrivals to form a separate new entity. The constant population shifts and the concomitant cultural exchange—both factors helped to produce close ethnic and cultural ties between neighboring regions—also influenced the economic development of the areas involved. Thus the introduction of metalworking into south-eastern Europe in the 4th millennium B.C. was connected with the beginning of the use of copper—and later bronze—for the production of weapons, tools and jewelry in Asia Minor. The Balkan peninsula was well placed in this respect because its mountain ranges were rich in deposits of copper, silver, gold and iron, although the latter was not made use of until 2,000 years later.

The increasing number of materials and techniques available made possible a greater diversity of products and thus strongly favored a process of cultural differentiation among the various regions, thereby raising the links and contacts between the neighboring cultural zones to a higher level of development.

This process of the formation and consolidation of cultural zones associated with particular national tribes was largely complete in the eastern Mediterranean and on the Balkan peninsula by the end of the Bronze Age, i. e. by the second half of the 2nd millennium B.C. The earliest written reference to the name "Thracians," which later became the generic term for the population living between the lower Danube and the Aegean, also dates from this time. It occurred in Homer's *Iliad*, an account of the legendary ten-year war waged by the Achaeans against Troy in which Thracian tribes fought on the side of the Trojans.

The Thracian people consisted of numerous individual tribes. The names of many of these tribes are known to us but not in every case their exact location, although they were certainly spread all over the Balkan peninsula and across parts of Asia Minor as well. They included the Odrysae, who inhabited an extensive area centring on the river Hebros (today Maritsa, in southern Bulgar-

2 Clay vessels from the late Stone or Chalcolithic Age (Cat. No. 3.1)

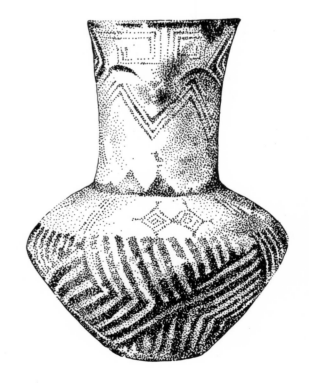

ia), and the Dardanae, who were situated partly on the Balkan peninsula and partly in the environs of Troy in Asia Minor. Among the other Thracian tribes were the Triballi in the north-west of present-day Bulgaria, the Moesians on the right bank of the Danube and the Getae, who settled south of the Danube delta in what is today Dobroudja. To the north of the Danube lived the Dacians; research into their ethnic identity has not yet been able to determine definitively whether they were an autonomous nation or a tribe of the Thracians. However, their culture and language of which, like that of the Thracians, only fragments are known to us, indicate a close affinity with the Thracians south of the Danube.

Homer's *Iliad* mentions a group of Thracian warriors led by a "king" called Rhesus. Homer depicts him as a great lover of pomp:

"The Thracians came on their own and lay separately
   from the others.
Their king was Rhesus, descended of Eioneus.
Ne'er did I see such great and magnificent steeds as his,
Whiter than snow and swift as the rushing wind.
His chariot was a splendid construction of gold and
   silver,
And as he approached we beheld with awe his mighty
   weapons of gold and silver.
Surely no mortal man could bear such arms,
They could only be intended for immortal gods."

(*The Iliad*, X, 434–441)

Although the term "king" used in such a poetic context should not be interpreted in its modern sense, its use nevertheless implies at least that Thracian society had already undergone a process of social differentiation, which is also reflected in the description of the ceremonial armor. This indicates that by the end of the 2nd millennium B.C. the social development among these tribes had reached a level which largely corresponded to that of Greece at this time. Among the Thracians the tribal chief or "king" also acted as high priest, and during this era earthly rulers were frequently placed on a par with gods or heroes. The mythical singer Orpheus is thus said to have been a Thracian king living in this epoch, a period in which historical reality and legend cannot be separated. He is said to have opposed the influence which the wine-god Dionysus had on the Thracian people and was for this reason torn asunder by women belonging to his own tribe in an ecstatic frenzy. Later the priest-king Orpheus became the object of religious veneration and was also adopted by Greek mythology.

Among the Thracians, as indeed throughout the whole of the eastern Mediterranean area, it was the introduction of iron-working and the growing use of this metal in the manufacture of weapons and production instruments which laid the economic basis for the increasing social differentiation among the population. As a result of improved tools the whole level of social production was raised considerably, thereby creating an important prerequisite for the development of private property, which in turn brought about the formation of different social classes.

In the mountains situated on Thracian territory there were rich deposits of iron. These were of immense significance for the economic and thus the social development of the country during the 1st millennium B.C. At the very time when the Thracians were emerging as a single ethnic entity for the first time in history, certain preconditions were already apparent for a development which, a few centuries later, was to reach its climax in the formation of the Thracian state. We have no knowledge whatsoever of the details of this process or of historical events between the 10th and 7th/6th centuries B.C.

In view of this fact, the Thracian tombs acquire a special significance since they are the most important archaeological monuments from which we can elicit some information concerning the early Iron Age. In south-eastern Thrace, i.e. among only one or a few Thracian tribes, the so-called dolmens had by this time made their appearance—tombs made of large and scarcely worked slabs of stone. There were also burial chambers hewn directly into steep rock-faces. Both types of tomb were constructed with varying degrees of elaborateness, which can be considered a reflection of the social differences prevailing within the society of the time. These dolmens and rock-face tombs were always constructed in mountainous areas and were probably related to the Thracian practice of sun-worship.

From the 8th century B.C. onwards, with the beginning of Greek colonization, information concerning Thrace becomes more abundant again. Greek settlements appeared on the coast of the Aegean and, from around 650 B.C. onwards, on the west coast of the Black Sea. This colonizing movement was the work of the Greek city-states (poleis). Members of all strata of the population were involved, but the majority were small-scale peasant producers who in this way sought to escape from the economic pressure exerted by the big landowners. These arable farmers also determined the character of the autonomous colonies. They patterned their political organization on the example of the polis from which they came, and as a rule also brought the cult prevailing in the parent city with them. The vast majority of the colonies on the west coast of the Black Sea were founded by citizens of the trading city of Miletus in Asia Minor, and nearly all of the coastal towns which exist in that region today were founded by the Greek colonizers in the 7th and 6th centuries B.C.

In the course of time the colonies on the coasts of Thrace developed into important trading centers and contact points between Greece and the Thracians living in the hinterland of the coastal towns. The latter supplied the Greek traders with wood and charcoal, metals, salt and fish in exchange for pottery, metal objects, luxury goods, oil and wine. As a result of the intensification of this commerce, which was initially based on a barter system, and in accordance with the general trend in the eastern Mediterranean, minted coins were introduced as a standard medium of payment on the markets, and in the second half of the 6th century B.C. the first Thracian coins appeared (pl. 4).

The late 6th and early 5th century B.C. was a time of conflict between the Greeks and the Persians. Owing to its geographical position at the intersection of important lines of communication between east and west and south and north, the Balkan peninsula also was affected. On a number of occasions the Persians marshalled their forces there before marching against Europe. Thrace's traditionally good relations with the Persian empire were important in this respect, and for a time large areas populated by Thracians were annexed to the Persian empire and placed under the jurisdiction of a satrap. The Persians found particular support among the Odrysae, whereas other Thracian tribes such as the Getae repeatedly fought against Persian rule.

Naturally, the decades of war against the Persians were reflected in Greek history-writing, which began at this time. In the process the Thracians became an object of consideration for the Greek historians and increasingly claimed their attention. The historical works of Herodotus and Thucydides are the most exhaustive reference sources of Thracian history we have, since the Thracians did not have a written language of their own. However, the information concerning Thrace provided by Greek historians should be treated with caution as they did not always report conditions in the region, which the Hellenes never regarded as more than a peripheral area, with sufficient insight and objectivity.

The Persian presence on the Balkan peninsula lasted from about 520 to 460 B.C. Their influence, especially on the social organization of the Odrysae, was considerable. Following the final defeat of the Persians in Greece and their subsequent withdrawal from the Balkan peninsula, the Odrysae attempted to fill the gap to some extent and claimed the leadership over the other Thracian tribes, which were by now showing initial signs of a state formation. Under the leadership of the Odrysian chieftain and later king Teres, who reigned from *c.* 460 to 440 B.C., a state structure emerged in the second quarter of the 5th century B.C. Here the social development of the Thracians, which had been underway since the late Bronze Age, reached its apogee and determined in large measure the character of the ensuing period. Politically, economically and culturally the Odrysian state, which maintained its hegemony until the start of the 3rd century B.C., may be regarded as the apex of Thracian society on the Balkan peninsula. Again there was a chronological parallel to events in neighboring Greece, which experienced its classical period during the 5th century B.C. before the existing social structures broke up in the wake of the following period of crisis.

In the absence of authentic evidence it is not possible to precisely determine the borders of the Odrysian realm at any time of its existence. Its center probably lay in what is now southern Bulgaria in the vicinity of the rivers Maritsa and Tundzha. It was along here that the important line of communication between the Aegean and the Thracian territories ran. One of the royal seats of the Odrysian kings was situated near the modern Bulgarian county-town of Yambol in the ancient city of Kabyle, which has been the subject of archaeological investigation for many years.

Following the Persian pattern of state organization, the Odrysian system of rule comprised the king plus several subordinate "paradynasts," who themselves established smaller residential and administrative seats within their areas of jurisdiction. On his tours of inspection around his scattered lands the king also made temporary stays in these town-like settlements.

During the phase of ethnic consolidation the mass of the Thracian population were small farmers who lived in unfortified rural settlements in the environs of the palaces of the "paradynasts" or of other members of the aristocracy. They had to perform military service as foot soldiers whereas the members of the upper class rode into battle on horseback. The cavalry was the main instrument of armed force of the Odrysae.

It was also due to Persian influence that the Odrysae had more highly developed tactical and technical methods of waging war at the beginning of the 5th century B.C. than the other Thracian tribes. With the help of his army the Odrysian king Teres was able to considerably extend the area of land under his control and to strengthen his state both internally and externally. Further expansion towards the west and south-west, under his son and successor Sitalces (*c.* 435 to 424 B.C.) created sources of friction with the interests of Athens in those regions. However, the Athenians were also intent on maintaining friendly relations with their Thracian neighbors, and they agreed to guarantee a steady source of tax revenue to the Thracians from members of the Delian League.

Under Sitalces and Seuthes I (424 to 410 B.C.), his nephew and successor, the political power of the Odrysian state attained its highpoint. In the struggle for supremacy in Greece between Athens and Sparta, which culminated in the Peloponnesian War, the Odrysian state fought on the side of Athens and was able to strengthen its own position as a result of the weakened situation of the Greek *poleis*. A kind of political equilibrium emerged between the Odrysae, the Delian League and the Persian empire.

Seuthes I was killed in 410 B.C. during the fighting between the Odrysae and the Triballi, another Thracian tribe, in which the Odrysae suffered a defeat. His death signalled the start of a phase of domestic political upheavals. His lawful successor Medokos (410 to 386 B.C.) was at first challenged for the throne by a nephew of Seuthes I.

The usurper, who became known as Seuthes II, was able to assert his rule for a time with the aid of Greek soldiers led by the historian Xenophon (c. 430 to 354 B.C.), who made a full report of the events and in doing so painted a detailed picture of Thracian life. Later, Seuthes recognized the authority of Medokos. Under Medokos' successor Hebryzelmos (386 to 383 B.C.) the good relations between the Odrysae and Athens continued. In 383 B.C. he was toppled by Kotys; the latter was king of the Odrysae until the year 359 and during this time helped to further strengthen the Odrysian state. The good relations with Athens which initially existed were reflected by the fact that he married his daughter to an Athenian, an action born of his desire to exploit the continuing domestic Greek struggles for his own ends. Conflict later arose between Kotys I and Athens, and in attempting to extend his power to the Greek coastal towns and thus gain open access to the sea for his realm the Thracian king was killed by Greek colonizers, who were consequently feted by Athens as saviours.

Although relations with Athens later improved again and the political significance of the Odrysian state increased once more, the death of Kotys I marked the start of the final decline of the Odrysian state.

From the 4th century B.C. onwards the Macedonian empire began to consolidate its power in the Aegean. The advance of the Macedonians was accompanied by the realization of the tendency towards the formation of a territorial state, which signified a loosening of the old *polis* structure. As a result of their close proximity both to Macedonia and to Greece, the Odrysae and the independent Thracian tribes were drawn into the struggle for supremacy within Greece at an early stage.

King Philip II of Macedon (359 to 336 B.C.) exploited the divisions among the Thracian "paradynasts" by conquering the southern part of the realm, which he did in 341 B.C., to rid himself of a serious threat and at the same time to gain access for his own state to the rich deposits of ore in the Thracian mountains. He then formed an alliance with the Getae living in north-eastern Thrace in order to protect himself against possible attacks from the Scythians in the north. But Philip was unable to subjugate the Triballi and it was left to his son and successor Alexander III, the Great (336 to 323 B.C.), to realize his father's ambition.

Since the neutralization of Thrace was basically merely a stepping stone as far as the ambitious schemes of the Macedonian king were concerned, it is not surprising that Macedonian influence there was kept to a bare minimum. At Philip's behest the town of Pulpudeva at the former core of the Odrysian state was lavishly expanded and given the name Philippopolis (today Plovdiv). The town was to represent Macedonian power in the area without, however, actually exercising it, for the institutions of the Odrysian realm remained formally intact. In reality, though, the Odrysae lost their former preeminence in Thrace, and the Macedonian conquest unleashed a political and social crisis in Thrace from which the country never recovered.

After the death of Alexander the Great his former general Lysimachus (323 to 281 B.C.) became the ruler of Thrace. In the wake of the political confusion which accompanied the disintegration of Alexander's world empire into individual states *(diadochoi)*, Seuthes III, who still held the title of king of the Odrysae, attempted to reestablish the realm. After a lengthy struggle he was victorious, and in 314 B.C. Lysimachus had to formally acknowledge him as king. However, in 305 B.C. Lysimachus himself adopted the title of king.

Seuthes III displayed his power as king of the Odrysae by establishing a royal residence which, adopting the Macedonian custom, he named Seuthopolis (in the vicinity of the modern town of Kazanluk). The remains of this town were flooded to make way for the Georgi Dimitrov reservoir, but not before a thorough archaeological investigation had been carried out. The town was laid out along Greek-Hellenistic lines with a sym-

Page 13

3 Funeral wake. Mural
painting from the domed
tomb near Kazanluk
(Cat. No. 1.13)

4 Coins of Thracian
kings (Cat. No. 3.11)
top left: Seuthes III
(324–311 B.C.)
top right: Kotys I
(383–359 B.C.)
bottom left: Teres II
(348 B.C.)
bottom right: Amadokos
(359–351 B.C.)

bottom: Sparadokos
(*c.* 424 B.C.)

5 Appliqué of gold foil in
the form of a bull from the
Eneolithic necropolis near
Varna (Cat. No. 1.1.2)

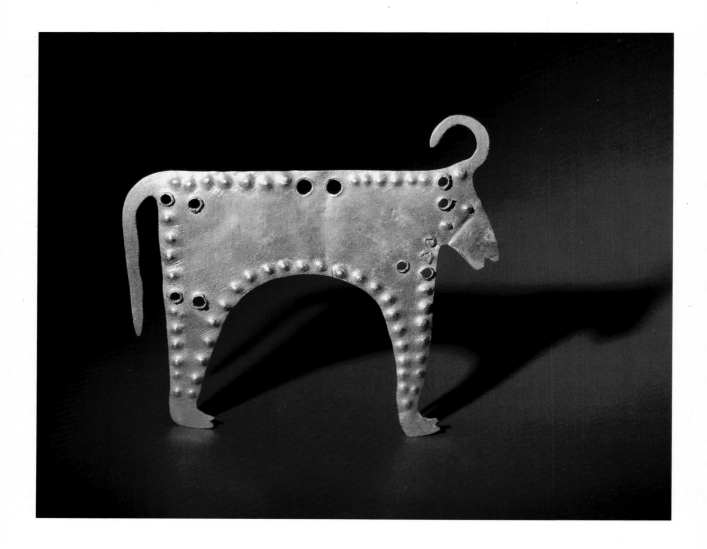

6 Gold foil covering for a scepter (Cat. No. 1.1.4)

7 Set of gold vessels from Vulchitrun (Cat. No. 2.2)
8 Large cymbal, gold with silver stripes (Cat. No. 2.2.4)

9 Triple offering vessel
(Cat. No. 2.2.6)
10 Decorated handle of
a *krater* (Cat. No. 2.2.1)

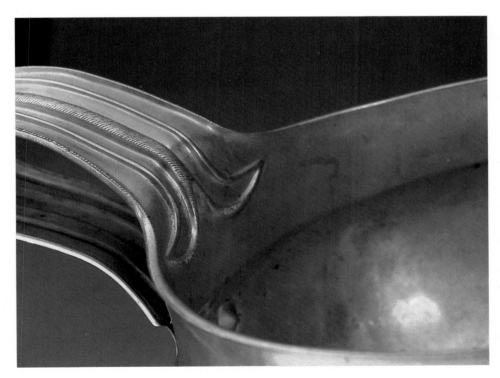

11 Bronze matrix with
animal friezes from Gur-
chinovo (Cat. No. 3.6)

12 Parcel-gilt silver *phiale*,
unusual in that it is decorated with human masks
(Cat. No. 2.8.1)

13 Gold *phiale* from Atanasovo (Cat. No 2.4)
14 Gold *phiale* from the treasure of Kasichene (Cat. No. 2.3)

15 Silver *phiale* with gilt medallion from the grave mound at Vratsa (Cat. No. 1.10.3)

16 Silver *phiale* with double wall from a grave mound near Boukyovtsi (Cat. No. 1.5.1)

17 Silver *phiale* from Vladinya (Cat. No. 2.7)

18 Set of silver vessels from Golyama Brestnitsa (Cat. No. 2.13)

19 Gold jar from the grave mound at Vratsa (Cat. No. 1.10.1)

20 Silver *phiale* with gilt relief of a horseman from the treasure of Yakimovo (Cat. No. 2.12)

21 Persian amphora, silver and parcel-gilt, from a barrow near Douvanli (Cat. No. 1.3.1)

22 Handle of the silver amphora from Douvanli in the form of a griffin, fitted with a pouring hole (Cat. No. 1.3.1)

23 *Rhyton* in the form of a deer's head from a barrow at Rozovets (Cat. No. 1.9)

24 *Rhyton* terminating in a horse *protome* from a grave mound near Douvanli (Cat. No. 1.3.4)

Following page

25 Three silver jars from the 4th century B.C. (Cat. Nos. 1.10.2; 1.10.4; 1.10.9)

metrical street network (pl. **26**). The individual buildings also reflected Greek influence. On the other hand, another aspect was of Persian origin. This was the principle according to which the royal palace was situated at the edge of a walled town but was then further fortified against the residential quarters by a second defensive wall. This late Thracian settlement thus combined elements of both Greek and Persian town planning.

Near Seuthopolis a domed tomb, which also dates from the reign of Seuthes III, was discovered in which the round burial chamber and connecting passage had been adorned with wall paintings in fresco technique (pl. **3**). In all probability the paintings, which depict a scene from a wake and funeral games, were done by a Greek artist on behalf of a Thracian client. The urban lay-out of Seuthopolis and the tomb of Kazanluk both show clearly that life in the Odrysian kingdom retained a certain independence even under Macedonian rule.

Under these circumstances the death of Lysimachus, who fell in 281 B.C., could have meant the regaining of political autonomy for the Thracians. But a new danger arose in the third quarter of the 3rd century B.C.: Celtic hordes emerged from the west and advanced across the Balkan peninsula in the course of their offensive against Greece and Asia Minor, where they were only defeated several decades later by the Pergamenes. After a series of successful battles against the Thracian population the Celts settled in the south-east of the country where they founded a realm of their own with its capital at Tylis. This town has still not been located, but it probably lay in the vicinity of the Strandzha mountains (in south-eastern Bulgaria). In fact, there are few archaeological traces of the Celts to be found south of the Danube, whereas their influence on the cultural development of the Dacians north of the Danube is unmistakable.

Celtic presence on the Balkan peninsula lasted some 60 years before the Thracians succeeded in expelling them around the year 216 B.C. However, Thracian society in general had been so severely weakened by Macedonian rule, the subsequent struggles with the Galatians and the increasing domestic political conflicts which followed the death of Kotys I in 359 B.C. that even after the withdrawal of the Celts it was never again able to regain its national unity.

Just as, during the Neolithic period and the Bronze Age, the Balkan peninsula's geographical location at the junction of the main lines of communication between east and west and south and north had been a decisive prerequisite for the formation and consolidation of the Thracian nation, so it continued to have a more or less direct bearing on the course of the country's historical development in the 1st millennium B.C. Thrace lay within the orbit of both Persia and Greece, and influences from these two directions stimulated both its economic (e.g. via the Greek colonies) and its political development (e.g. through the adoption of forms of state organization taken from the Persian empire). At the same time Thrace was also directly involved in all the major military conflicts of the time, since it was either used as an assembly point by the various belligerent parties prior to the fighting (as in the Greek-Persian wars of the 6th and 5th centuries B.C.) or else was an area in which the interests of the opposing forces overlapped (as in the encounters between Greece and Macedonia in the 4th century B.C.). Thus the Thracians were always closely involved during the 1st millennium B.C. in the historical developments in the political centers of the eastern Mediterranean.

After the Thracian state had lost its erstwhile significance in the 3rd century B.C., several small statelets formally existed within its former boundaries, although in fact they were part of the weakened Macedonian empire. For this reason the Thracians were drawn, from the 2nd century B.C. onwards, into the struggle which the increasingly powerful Roman state was waging for hegemony in this region. In the decisive battle between Rome and Macedonia in the year 168 B.C. Thracian soldiers fought as part of the Macedonian army.

Rome's victory signalled a new historical epoch for Thrace and for the other nations in the region. King Kotys III signed a separate peace treaty with the Romans, so that from then on the Odrysian kings were mere clients or vassals of Rome, i.e. they were dependants of Rome. Subsequently Thracians crop up on several occasions in Roman records, mostly as slaves. In earlier times Thracians are known to have sold members of their family or tribe to Greece. But now the slave trade expanded further, since the Roman econo-

26 Plan of the Thracian royal residence of Seuthopolis

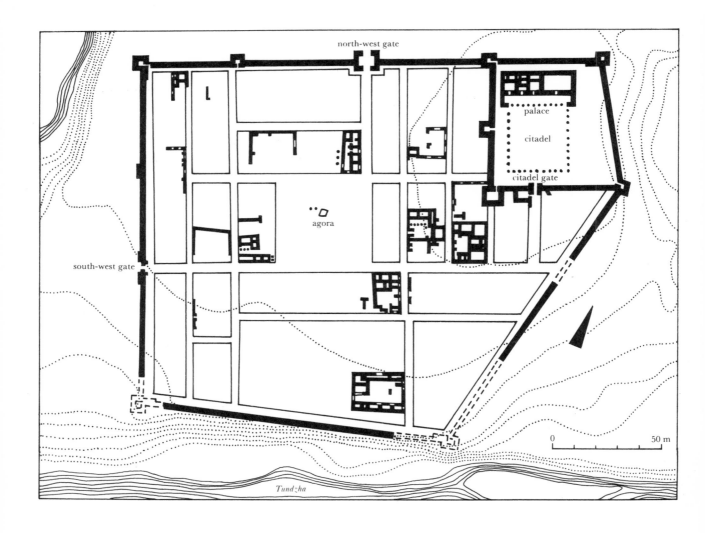

north-west gate

palace

citadel

citadel gate

agora

south-west gate

0   50 m

Tundzha

my was much more strongly based on slave labor than that of the Greeks. In the mines and among the gladiators there were large numbers of Thracians, of whom the most famous was Spartacus, the leader of the biggest slave uprising in antiquity (74 to 71 B.C.).

From the 2nd century B.C. onwards the focus of political developments within the territory populated by Thracian tribes—the area stretching from the Carpathian basin to the Aegean coast—shifted more and more to the north. The agents of this process were the Geto-Dacians. During the apogee of the Odrysian state the Dacians did not play a very significant political role. It was only after the Celtic invasions that their historical importance increased.

In the 1st century B.C. the Dacian leader Burebista (82 to 44 B.C.) founded an autonomous state in the Orastie mountains (today in north-western Romania) and within a short time had succeeded in uniting most of the Dacians under his leadership. With his army he even intervened directly in Roman politics when, in the 50s, he sided with Pompey in the civil war against Caesar. The latter planned a retaliatory campaign against the Dacians after defeating Pompey, but he was prevented from realizing this by his assassination in 44 B.C. At around the same time Burebista was also killed, whereupon his realm disintegrated again; only in the former heartlands of the Orastie mountains did some kind of state structure continue to exist.

While the Odrysian client state was transformed into a Roman province under Emperor Claudius (A.D. 41 to 54), the Dacians carried on their bitter struggle for independence. In A.D. 85/86, when Domitian was the emperor (A.D. 81 to 96), they invaded the Roman province of Moesia. The invasion unleashed four years of bloody warfare until the Romans, despite their military superiority, had to call a halt in A.D. 89. Meanwhile the Dacians had a new king in Decebalus (A.D. 87 to 106). He managed once again to unite the Dacians under his leadership. He took advantage of the assistance which the Romans gave him after A.D. 89 to secretly build up a great army against them. Consequently Emperor Trajan (A.D. 98 to 117) felt obliged to do battle with the Da-

cians under Decebalus, although he had to wage two hard wars (in A.D. 101/102 and A.D. 105/106) before he was able to conquer the country and incorporate it into the Roman empire as a province.

At the end of the second war Decebalus committed suicide, prompted by the ignominy of defeat. Trajan exploited his victory over the Dacians with an unprecedented display of political propaganda. He built a forum in Rome in the center of which a 33 meter-high column was erected. The latter was then covered with a spiral frieze measuring 200 m in length on which the most important events of the two wars were depicted.

One of the main battles during these two wars took place in what is today Dobroudja (near Adamclisi in south-eastern Romania), and here Trajan likewise set up a victory column as well as a cenotaph for the fallen Roman soldiers. He also founded there the town of Tropaeum Traiani. Both in the new province of Dacia and throughout the entire eastern Balkans the Emperor strengthened Roman influence by devoting particular attention to urban development. This included the establishment of two more towns south of the Danube whose names were also reminders of the Roman victory over the Dacians: Nicopolis ad Istrum ("victory-town on the Danube", near Turnovo in northern Bulgaria) and Nicopolis ad Nestum ("victory-town on the Mesta", in south-western Bulgaria).

Only 170 years after their spectacular arrival on the Balkan peninsula the Romans had to surrender Dacia, which was the last province they acquired there, whereas the provinces south of the Danube remained part of the Roman empire until the time of the Slavic and proto-Bulgarian settlements in the 6th and 7th centuries. Yet in the Dacian areas the Romans had a more profound impact on cultural development than in those areas populated by the Thracians. Even today this is still noticeable, e.g. in the fact that in medieval Romania the Slavic language was unable to assert itself against its Romance rival. South of the Danube, Thracian traditions from pre-Roman times survived in a few inaccessible mountainous regions and were directly subsumed into medieval Slavic-Bulgarian culture.

Discovery of the Oldest Finds of Gold Objects at Varna

2

A most important find, both in terms of its material value and its cultural and historical significance, was made in recent years at the more than 5,000 year-old necropolis at Varna. Machines digging up a site in the industrial quarter of Varna, Bulgaria's largest port, in 1972 unearthed some gold objects which turned out to be burial accessories. An archaeological investigation was immediately set in train. By 1982 over 200 graves, which had formed part of a cemetery set on a terrace directly on the north bank of Lake Varna, had been investigated. In addition to various stone and copper utensils around 2,000 gold objects were found, with a total weight of 5.4 kg. However, the importance of the discovery lay not so much in the number of objects found as in the fact that it was the oldest find on this scale ever made on the Balkan peninsula. The cemetery was laid out between 3200 and 3000 B.C. at a time when the use of stone was increasingly being supplemented by metals—at first mainly copper—for the manufacture of tools and weapons. For this reason the term Stone-Copper Age or Chalcolithic Age was given to this epoch.

The good state of preservation and wide variety of the objects from the necropolis at Varna have enabled us to gather vital information concerning various aspects of the life of the people in the 4th millennium B.C. The metal artifacts found without doubt represent the apex of technical and technological development of the time. The majority of the objects consist of cylindrical beads fashioned from gold foil. There are also a number of rings; these include finger-rings, bracelets, chain links and ear-pendants; several bangles and various flat and convex plaques (pl. **27**) which were forms of jewelry and were sewn onto clothing which is no longer extant.

The most prominent among these very simple ornaments are items which bear the realistic outline of a bull (pl. **5**) and others which depict in highly stylized form a horned ram's head. All these objects consist of gold with only a small admixture of silver and platinum. This gold was mined at unidentified locations in the eastern Mediterranean, transported to the western coast of the Black Sea and there turned into jewelry in local workshops. The deposits of gold lying in the mountains of the Balkan peninsula itself were not mined until later times. Thus in the 4th millennium B.C. there were already clearly discernible trading contacts between the inhabitants of Asia Minor and those of the Balkans, and the latter had by this stage also acquired the know-how for processing gold. The finds from the necropolis at Varna, though the most important, are by no means the only discoveries of treasure dating from this period which have been found on Bulgarian territory.

During this early era of metalworking the raw materials were made use of in their natural form. The same was true of copper—which gave the epoch its name —which was mined using simple means and, to begin with, worked in unalloyed form. Although the use of copper objects had certain advantages compared to those of stone, the low level of productivity associated with their manufacture meant that for a time stone implements continued to be produced. Thus the copper axes and needles found in the graves at Varna and at other sites must once have been almost as valuable as the gold jewelry.

The finds from the necropolis at Varna provide much other information besides such economic facts. The tombs which were investigated fall into several different

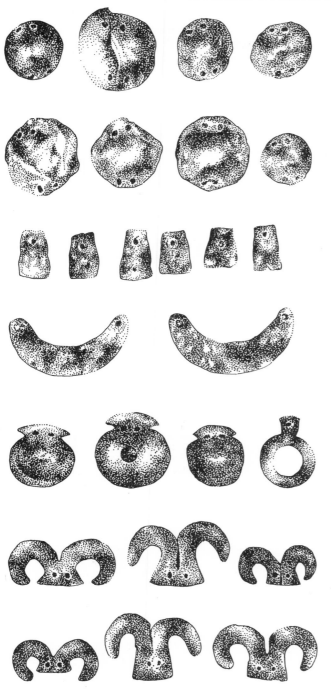

types. Firstly, there are the burial pits in which the legs of the deceased are drawn up to the chest, the so-called contracted burials. Although this method of burial is typical of the Chalcolithic cemeteries on the Balkan peninsula, only a few scattered examples were found at Varna.

On the other hand, graves in which the corpse was fully stretched out, with the head normally facing north-east, occur here more frequently than at other sites. And this is the only burial site so far discovered on which symbolic graves have been found, i. e. graves in which no body was actually buried. Such graves, known as cenotaphs, were dug for men who, for example, had achieved noteworthy deeds for their native region or tribe, possibly having fallen on some distant battlefield.

Representing the head of the dead hero lay a clay mask on which the eyes, mouth and teeth were indicated by gold plaques; it was further decorated with a gold diadem and gold earrings, and at the place where the neck would have been were little gold amulets (pl. **28**). In other respects the cenotaphs were adorned in the same fashion as the graves containing burials.

Some of the graves at Varna contain a remarkable amount of gold jewelry, while others are more modestly adorned. Among those with a wealth of ornamentation, a number contained some unusual objects. Thus some of the corpses bore a diadem of gold foil above the forehead, a decorative gold plate on the chest and a scepter (pl. **6**) with an axe-like upper part of gold or sometimes copper or stone—an indication of the high value of all three materials. The wooden handle of these scepters was covered with gold leaf. These objects were badges of power and signified that the deceased had been a tribal prince, a priest or a military chieftain—in fact, at this stage of social development all three offices were commonly held by one and the same person. In any event, the finds from the necropolis at Varna prove that by 3000 B.C. the degree of social differentiation among the people living in the eastern part of the Balkan peninsula was already quite pronounced.

The finds in the graves at Varna also provide some answers to questions concerning the religion and culture of the inhabitants of the Balkan peninsula during the Chalcolithic Age. Certain religious notions are suggested by the amulets of gold foil with which the death masks in a number of symbolic graves were decorated, as indeed by the presence of several cult idols made of bone, which occurred only in these graves which contained no corpse. In both cases human figures are depicted in a highly stylized form which were intended to protect the deceased in the next world. People clearly believed in a life after death, for along with the corpse they buried idols representing the unnameable powers which also determined the fate of the individual during his earthly existence. This belief in a life after death also gave rise to the need to provide the deceased with objects for his personal use.

According to the religious conceptions of the people living during this epoch, these powers were closely bound up with natural phenomena on which depended the growth and ripening of their grain, the health of both wild and domesticated animals and, ultimately, their own existence. This fertility cult, especially the idealized portrayals of the bull and the ram's head, was directly related to the economic basis of existence at this stage of social development. It provides some idea of the problems with which the arable farmers and cattle breeders were faced in their struggle with Nature.

In considering the finds from the necropolis at Varna there is one important aspect which we have not yet touched on, namely their place within the development of art in the eastern part of the Balkan peninsula. The ability to fashion metals into objects of art presupposes an advanced division of labor within the community. Only when the level of development of the productive forces made this possible could individual members of the community, at least on a temporary basis, be released from the task of producing the goods that were directly necessary for day-to-day existence so that they could acquire the requisite special knowledge and skills for manufacturing metal objects. The artists of the 4th millennium B.C. reduced the natural forms known to them to the bare essentials, so that at times the object depicted is barely recognizable. Such extreme stylization, reduced to very basic geometric forms, characterizes the humanoid bone figures and ram's head plaques, as well as the gold amulets which are scarcely

Preceding page

27 Gold foil appliqués from the Chalcolithic necropolis near Varna (Cat. No. 1.1.1)

28 Face mask of unbaked clay with gold trimmings (Cat. No. 1.1.3)

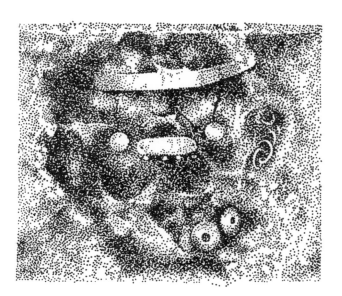

recognizable as anthropomorphic likenesses. Conversely there were also examples of much less stylized decoration such as the plaques of gold foil depicting bulls.

Both of these early artistic tendencies—the highly stylized idols and amulets and the more naturalistic bovine figures—were closely associated with the Nature/fertility cult. Similarly, the gold personal jewelry also had a precise social function: diadems, ceremonial breastplates and scepters all indicated the high social status of the owner.

The Hoard of Vulchitrun

3

The biggest find of gold treasure ever made in what was formerly Thrace was also the result of an accident. It was discovered near the village of Vulchitrun in the northern Bulgarian district of Pleven in December 1924 and has been housed ever since in the Archaeological Museum in Sofia. It consists of 13 items, is of high-carat gold and has a total weight of 12.425 kg (pl. **7**). The center-piece of the set is the *krater*, a vessel weighing over four kilograms in which, according to the ancient custom, the wine was mixed with water. It has an unusual shape for a metal vessel. The two handles were not added later but were moulded from the mouth of the vessels and secured to the shoulder by means of three rivets.

Similar handles adorn the smaller cups in the set. The surface of the *krater* is smooth and plain, but along the upper side of the band-like handles run three ridges; the middle one is broader than the other two and is scored with diagonal fluting (pl. **10**). The three rivets just below the lip and in line with the ridges form a second point of decoration.

Supplementing this large mixing vessel are four *kyathoi*: one larger and three smaller cups, each with a single handle. They are made in the same way as the *krater* and share the same design, including the looped handle emerging from the lip which is attached to the shoulder via three rivets. The decorative pattern on the handle of the larger cup is the same as that of the *krater*, while the handles of the smaller cups show only a single fluted ridge flanked by two rows of dots. In view of the identical decoration—the plainer design of the small *kyathoi* is due to their smaller size—the five vessels may be regarded as together forming a set.

The set is completed by seven gold disks (lids), two equally large and five smaller ones. They all have an onion-shaped knob on the upper surface. Whereas the smaller ones are devoid of decoration the two largest bear a pattern on their top sides consisting of very thin bands of silver worked into the surface (pl. **8**).

Originally there were eight disks in the set. These formed four pairs: three smaller ones and a large, decorated pair. This combination of three-plus-one also indicates that they formed an integral unit with the drinking vessels.

The triple vessel illustrated in plate **9** is the only example of its kind, both in the Vulchitrun find and among all known metal vessels from the Balkan peninsula. Nevertheless, with its tripartite structure it fits in neatly with the rest of the complex. It comprises three identical shallow, spoon-like or ovoid dishes with a fluted pattern whose undersides are connected by three tubes of electrum, an alloy of gold and silver. The upper, broader ends of the three individual components are connected by a system of electrum tubes with a common spout by means of which liquid could be poured into all three dishes simultaneously.

The Vulchitrun find is unique in its totality. Efforts to determine its date and function have been additionally hampered by the fact that no archaeological clues, such as the remains of a building, were found in the vicinity of the find which might have thrown some light onto the historical and cultural conditions under which the vessels were manufactured and later buried. Thus the date of manufacture put forward by the various experts varies from the 3rd millennium B.C. to the first half of the 1st millennium B.C. However, comparisons with clay vessels showed that, at the earliest, the *krater* and the *kyathoi* were made in the 13th or 12th century B.C., a date which therefore probably applies also to the disks and the triple vessel. Investigations have established that the gold employed was mined in the Carpathians in what is today Romania. The vessels themselves, however, were made in a Thracian workshop. The local craftsman was not only an accomplished master of the artistic side of his trade, he also possessed extensive technical knowledge, which can be seen both in the fine silver inlays on the two large disks and also in the way the electrum was worked.

The technical execution and artistic design of the set show that the Thracian craftsman was familiar with the work of contemporary fellow artists in neighboring Mycenae. In the second half of the 2nd millennium B.C. Mycenae had reached the zenith of its political and cultural development and maintained numerous contacts with other peoples, including the Thracians. The use of rivets to attach the handles to the *krater* and the *kyathoi*, and also the decoration of the two large disks with an endless undulating band, was based on Mycenaean precursors, and is thus an important indication of the date of manufacture of the Vulchitrun hoard.

Yet how was it possible for such a complete set of gold vessels, which for its owner represented a considerable treasure, to end up buried in the earth in a spot clearly far removed from the place where it was originally used? Only an external threat could have caused its owner or custodian to bury the treasure in a place where the uninitiated could never find it. Such a danger could either have been a local, direct one or else the result of a generally insecure historical situation. Several such hoards of treasure were found hidden in the broad plains on either side of the lower Danube between the Carpathians and the Balkan mountains. They were all hidden during the second half of the 2nd millennium B.C. at a time when the Balkans and the entire eastern Mediterranean were overrun by various tribes who traversed the area in search of new habitats. Encounters with the indigenous population were inevitable. In the course of these migrations, which lasted several centuries, the advanced Mycenaean civilization also perished. The legendary Trojan War and the destruction of Troy were also connected with these events. With these new settlements of large groups of people the ethnic composition of the populations affected began to alter, and there were also changes in their social and economic development. It was during this period of historical transition, when people were in constant fear for their lives, that the hoard at Vulchitrun was buried to prevent its loss or capture by the enemy.

A set of vessels of solid gold—what sort of person could have owned such a possession and what could have been its function? In view of the level of development of the productive forces and the standard of living possible at the time it is unlikely that it was a private possession or an object of everyday household use. The constantly recurring theme of the triad, which also features in a clay depiction of a ritual scene from the 4th millennium B.C., is worthy of note. Although it is not possible to precisely define the context in which the set was used and hence the function of each individual item therein, it is nevertheless fairly safe to say that the Vulchitrun hoard was employed for special ceremonial rituals. Possibly it was used in the following manner: a sacrificial drink was mixed in the *krater*, part of which was then poured into the triple vessels. Owing to the ingenious system of tubes the three dishes were filled simultaneously. The priest was thus able to sacrifice to three gods at once without slighting or favoring any one of them since this, according to the prevailing beliefs, would have brought down their wrath on him. This ritual was accompanied by the sound of cymbals (the disks), with each of the three smaller pairs being dedicated to one particular deity. The two larger cymbals and the single large cup no doubt had some higher ceremonial function.

Vessels of Gold and Silver

4

Among the finds unearthed in what was formerly Thrace, either through accident or in the course of systematic archaeological excavations, there have been few examples of monumental art. The Thracians had no buildings comparable with, for instance, the temples of neighboring Greece, nor do we know of any large-scale Thracian sculptures. The concern to artistically depict the human being in all his multiplicity, which was such a crucial factor in the work of the Greek artists, was never a prime concern of the Thracians. Sculptures and monumental painting are found only in connection with tombs, and here there is such a strong foreign artistic influence, especially from the Greeks, that it may well be that Greek artists were directly employed to do the work, e.g. in the case of the frescoes in the vaulted tomb at Kazanluk.

Thracian art was much more concerned with the decoration of objects. To this end clay and precious metals were their favorite materials. This again highlights the fact that contacts between the Balkan peninsula and western Asia existed from a very early period. The introduction of metals into the production process in the 4th to 3rd millennium B.C. was closely followed by the development of techniques for working them into artistic objects. Thus within Persian civilization toreutics—the cold-working of precious metals—had already reached a high level of development. Eastern influences on the production of metal objects in Thrace, which had endured throughout the Bronze Age, gained even greater significance for Thracian craftsmanship when, in the 6th century B.C., the Persian empire extended its political power to the coastal towns of Asia Minor and across broad areas of the Balkan peninsula itself. This cultural influence expressed itself both in the adoption of Persian stylistic elements and in the direct import of articles from Persian workshops. However, when the Persians were forced to withdraw from Europe in the first half of the 5th century B.C. these cultural contacts also waned, and Thracian art at this time increasingly began to show traces of Greek influence, a phenomenon which in turn was related to the blossoming power of Athens in the eastern Mediterranean.

The geographical location of the Thracian territories among the different cultural zones of the eastern Mediterranean provided a strong impulse for the development of artistic craftsmanship. Toreutics was equally well developed and widespread as bronze-casting. Embossing was the principal method used in the manufacture of vessels from silver or gold foil. A matrix was made of wood or metal and its shape and contours then transferred to the gold or silver foil by hammering. At Gurchinovo in north-eastern Bulgaria a bronze cast was discovered which probably dates back to the 5th century B.C. and was used in stamping reliefs onto metal goblets (pl. 11). It has a handle on one side and depicts two animal friezes of different sizes. The larger of the two shows four animals: in the center a collapsing stag with its head turned towards a small lion which is attacking it from behind, on the left a horned griffin and on the right a bird—possibly an eagle—with its head turned towards the central pair. The motif of the bird's head with a big eye and powerful beak reoccurs in various guises on the frieze: highly stylized versions can be seen amidst the figures of the main frieze, while the tines of the stag's antlers and the horns of the griffin are also depicted as birds' heads. Taken together, the griffin's horns, the attacking lion, the stag's antlers and the bird's head form a decorative border to the frieze.

Beneath the moulded line which forms the lower edge of the main frieze is a smaller scene portraying a row of animals: lions, both *couchant* and *passant*, a wild boar, a unicorn and a stag. The decorative design of the manes and antlers is once again apparent, though in a much simpler form than on the main frieze.

The frequent depiction of animals, sometimes real and sometimes fabulous ones, and the strongly ornamental and hence unreal style of whole figures or of details was a basic feature of Thracian art and one which it shared with the cultures of other nations such as the Scythians, although we should not necessarily infer from this that they influenced one another. It would be more appropriate to seek the common roots of both the Thracian and the Scythian Animal Style in Persian art, where the parallels are most striking. More will be said in another context about the significance of the Animal Style in Thracian art, for although there were indeed vessels which were decorated with such animal designs, as the bronze matrix shows, there were relatively few of them.

An even more unusual decorative motif for a metal vessel was the double row of parcel-gilt female heads on a deep bowl of silver foil (pl. **12**). This vessel is part of a set which was probably buried as treasure in the northern foreland of the Balkan mountains during the series of military conflicts with the Macedonians in the second half of the 4th century B.C. A bronze or wooden cast of the type discussed above was used to produce the frieze. The broad facial features and the diadems, which should be understood as symbols of divinity, indicate that this vessel was manufactured by a local Thracian craftsman.

Phialai. Originally the *phiale* was a shallow dispensing bowl with an everted mouth. On the base was a raised boss which symbolized the mythical *omphalos*—the center of the earth—and which also made the vessel easier to handle during the presentation of the sacrificial drink.

As a vessel used for ritual purposes the *phiale* possessed particular significance for the Thracians and was largely made of precious metals. A relatively early ex-

ample was found quite by accident near Sofia together with a copper pot and a clay bowl (pl. **14**). This *phiale* was made of gold foil between 1000 and 700 B.C. It is decorated with radial fluting emanating from a circle containing studs connected by dotted lines, with the flat *omphalos* at the center. Although it strikes us as somewhat crude the *phiale* bears what was to become the characteristic decorative principle for this type of vessel, with a series of lines radiating out from a central boss.

A similar bowl, also of gold foil, was found in southern Bulgaria and probably dates to the 5th century B.C. (pl. **13**). In this case there is no additional decoration of the *omphalos* and a stylized pattern of alternating gadrooned lotus leaves and lotus buds has replaced the straight fluting.

The majority of the *phialai* found on Thracian territory were wrought of silver foil. The raw material employed came mostly from deposits in the Thracian mountains. The list of objects discovered in a burial mound included two silver *phialai* which were used in the burial ritual for a sacrificial offering and then placed in the grave next to the corpse along with silver plaques. One of these *phialai* (pl. **16**) is an almost classical example of this type of vessel. The interior of the bowl is smooth, the only decoration being a wreath of tonguelike ornaments around the raised *omphalos*. The outside of the everted mouth is also smooth, while the lower part of the bowl is enveloped by a second layer of silver with a chasework pattern.

The *phialai*, as indicated by their common occurrence in graves, were closely associated with the funeral rites of the Thracians. Their basic form rarely changed but there were a variety of production techniques and decorative motifs. One sacrificial bowl found near the village of Vladinya in northern Bulgaria (pl. **17**) is of a simpler technical design with a very different decor from the one described above. The body of the vessel consists of a single sheet of silver foil and the unusual cruciform pattern surrounding the *omphalos* has been directly embossed onto the wall of the vessel. Once again the broad rim is devoid of decoration.

The *omphalos* of some *phialai* was decorated with a carved medallion. In such cases the ritualistic associations are particularly apparent since the pictures usually have a religious character. A silver *phiale* found in a sumptuously adorned female burial in the Mogilanska mound in Vratsa (north-western Bulgaria) bears a gilt medallion on the *omphalos* depicting the head of the goddess Aphrodite (pl. **15**). Around the head are two wreaths and a beaded band. The vessel has the usual radial fluting and the line of demarcation between the decorated body of the vessel and the plain lip is accentuated by an ornamental border. The *phiale* was made in a Greek workshop in the first half of the 4th century B.C. but its nonstandard form indicates the particular taste of the Thracian client for whom it was made. This synthesis of Greek and Thracian elements in a way reflects the social and political conditions under which the vessel was produced, since this was a time during which the Odrysian state, having consolidated itself, enjoyed friendly relations with its Greek neighbors. Commercial and cultural contacts between the two areas flourished, and numerous *objets d'art* were produced in Greek workshops for aristocratic Thracian clients whose tastes and luxurious life styles emulated those of the Greek nobility.

A simply made silver bowl dating from the 1st century B.C. was one of a number of silver vessels found near Yakimovo in north-western Bulgaria (pl. **20**). On its outer surface is the figure of a horseman. The gilding has been inexpertly done. Everything is in profile except for the horseman's head, which presents a frontal view. He is wearing long trousers, boots and a cloak after the fashion of Greek barbarians and is armed with a sword. His hair as well as the horse's hair and mane are indicated by striations. The bowl was made by a local Thracian toreut who based his design on products of Greek origin, although he did not fully master the art of perspective or the technique of gilding. Yet the theme depicted is very much a Thracian one: the Thracian Horseman, a central figure in Thracian religion and one which we shall comment on in greater detail in another context.

The Celtic invasions of the 3rd century B.C. and the subsequent rule of the Macedonians prevented any further autonomous social and cultural development in Thrace. And during the first centuries A.D., i.e. while Thrace was a Roman province, the products of Thracian artists were scarcely distinguishable from those from other parts of the Roman empire. The enormous difference between metal vessels made while Thrace was at its zenith and those dating from the Roman era is evident from a set of vessels of thick silver foil consisting of a large cylindrical bowl and five smaller vessels which each have a handle (pl. **18**). The bowl is unadorned apart from a dedication to the Thracian Horseman in Greek on the upper rim. It is repeated on the handle of one of the smaller vessels. The handles of the other four vessels are each decorated in a different way.

This set of silver vessels was found by chance in a vineyard on the northern slopes of the Balkan mountains. In the surrounding area numerous objects emanating from a Thracian settlement during the period of Roman rule have been and continue to be found. On this same site, which has not yet been systematically investigated, there was once a shrine of some kind to the Thracian Horseman. It was probably here that the very plain set of vessels was used during various ritual ceremonies.

Jars. Whenever a Thracian priest wanted to offer a libation from a *phiale* during a ritual ceremony, whenever a nobleman carried out some other similar ritual on a smaller scale, or whenever some important domestic or foreign activity of the state—whether it be the conclusion of peace, a declaration of war, the investiture of a ruler or the signing of treaties with other nations—necessitated a sacrifice to the gods, the *omphalos* bowl itself was not sufficient: other vessels were necessary for storing the consecrated liquid. This function was largely fulfilled by jars which were also made of precious metals—usually of silver but sometimes also of gold. Yet it is relatively rare that this functional interconnection between *phialai* and jars is apparent from common features of their design or decoration (one such exception being the set of ritual vessels from Vulchitrun with the uniform decoration of the handle of the large mixing vessel and the four smaller *kyathoi*). Frequently, however, several bowls and jars are found on the same site, indicating that they belong together.

In spite of the many individual variations in design, it is nevertheless clear that underlying the form and decoration of the jars were the same artistic principles and stylistic influences, stemming from Persian and Greek art, as applied in the case of the *phialai*. Thus the lower part of the neck of a silver jar which was among the grave goods of a burial under the Mogilanska mound in Vratsa (pl. **25**, right) bears a gadrooned ovule pattern also found on many *phialai*. Band ornaments decorate the vessel's shoulder, rim of the mouth and handle edges. The handle is attached to the wall of the jar at the lower end in the form of a palmette. The jar's slim and elegant form and the type of decoration suggest the influence of Greek art. At the time when the tomb was laid out—i.e. in the third quarter of the 4th century B.C.—Greece and Thrace were on good terms with one another, especially as the two nations were under an equal threat from the Macedonians. The troubled times which accompanied Macedonian expansion under King Philip II and his son Alexander the Great caused valuable objects to be buried in many areas of Thrace.

The smaller, rather squat silver jar from the same grave mound in Vratsa (pl. **25**, left) was made by a local Thracian craftsman. Its whole body is covered with fluting which terminates at the shoulder in a tongued pattern; the shoulder, neck, mouth and handle are all devoid of decoration.

From the same find comes the handle-less jar with a conical body (pl. **25**, background). In form and design it resembles a pine-cone. The pine-cone was long regarded as a symbol of fertility in the eastern Mediterranean, and its scaly surface became a widespread decorative motif with hardly any relevance to its original significance. The smooth neck is marked off from the shoulder by a double line while an arcaded pattern appears on the lip.

In the same barrow at Mogilanska near Vratsa under which several very lavishly adorned graves from the 4th century B.C. lay concealed, a small jar of gold foil only 9 cm high and weighing a mere 240 g was found (pl. **19**), which merits special attention because of the representational scene depicted on its wall. This shows two winged quadrigae the wings of which meet at the back beneath the handle to form a symmetrical contrast around the wall of the vessel. Each chariot is driven by the Thracian equivalent of the Greek god Apollo. The divine driver, chariot wheels and wings have a somewhat clumsy appearance while the line of four horses with their decorated bridles make a more convincing impression. On the far side of the vessel between the two teams is a palmette, and a frieze of palmettes encircles the shoulder. The base and lip are decorated with ovules, while the handle is shaped in the form of a so-called "knot of Heracles," a complicated bow which the Greeks were accustomed to use to tie their belts.

The Thracian goldsmith must have been familiar with the portrayal of figures on metal vessels from Greek works. Greek influence is also visible in the winged quadriga driven by the god and in the form of the handle, though the artistic execution of the piece suggests that a Thracian workshop was responsible. Throughout antiquity the Thracians were famed as riders and connoisseurs of horses, and animal motifs were always immensely popular subjects in Thracian art. It is also notable that on the jar from Vratsa the horses occupy by far the largest amount of space while the chariots and the deities are disproportionately small.

In the 6th century B.C. the Thracians, who at this period still had no unified state structure, were ruled for a time by the Persians whose influence lingered on and manifested itself in numerous aspects of the state organization of the Thracian empire which finally arose under the Odrysian kings in the 5th century B.C. In the realm of culture, Persian prototypes, which reached Thrace directly via trade routes or as presents, were of great importance. An example of one such imported Persian product was discovered in a grave mound near Douvanli in southern Bulgaria dating from the early years of the 5th century B.C. (pl. **21**). This amphora of parcel-gilt silver foil has a fluted lower part surmounted by a frieze of palmettes and lotus blossoms which appears again on the shoulder in inverted form. An ovule border separates the wall of the vessel from the plain neck.

A characteristic feature of Persian-Achaemenid art was to design handles in the form of fabulous creatures, in this instance as horned lion-griffins (pl. **22**). On the back of one of the creatures is a spout, so that the vessel could either be used directly to offer a libation or else in conjunction with the drinking horns *(rhyta)*.

Drinking vessels. Both Persian and Greek influence is apparent in the style of the drinking vessels made from precious metals which have been found in Thrace. These zoomorphic *rhyta* originated in the Orient before spreading to Greece where they underwent a formal and independent stylistic development.

Two basic forms of these idiosyncratic drinking vessels are known to us from Thrace. One group was depicted as animal heads. Plate **23**, for example, shows a realistic portrayal of a deer's head. Surmounting the head is a straight neck, as in the case of the jars. The neck was sometimes adorned with reliefs. The deer-head *rhyton*, which was made in the early 4th century B.C., shows a scene with a Dionysian theme: in the middle a silenus, carrying a *kantharos* full of wine on his shoulder, is flanked by two dancing satyrs. A creeper of ivy entwines all three figures. Dionysus, the Greek god of wine who, according to one version of the myth, came from Thrace, was also worshipped by the Thracians. The form in which his three companions are depicted is also taken from Greek art. Dionysian motifs used to adorn a *rhyton* were fully in keeping with its function as a wine goblet. The liquid was poured into the *rhyton* from above, and a small opening between the deer's flews allowed a thin trickle of wine to enter the partaker's mouth.

The other group of *rhyta* had a lower part in the form of an animal *protome* whose hind quarters then merge into a long, slightly curved funnel shape. The funnel bears grooves which become wider towards the mouth. Plate **24** shows a parcel-gilt silver *rhyton* found in a burial in the necropolis near Douvanli which dates back to around 400 B.C. It terminates in an equine *protome* of silver foil; the mane, hooves and the decorated neck-band of the horse are all gilt, as is a frieze of palmettes and lotus blossoms engraved on the upper rim of the vessel. On this *rhyton* the bung-hole is situated between the horse's forelegs.

The *rhyton* with the horse *protome* shows up Persian influence even more strongly than the deer-head *rhyton* in its entire appearance. At the same time, the vessel from Douvanli proves that Greek craftsmen were also familiar with this form, since the design of the horse clearly bears the mark of the Greek craftsman who made this drinking vessel for a Thracian client.

The metal vessels which have so far been unearthed together provide a comprehensive insight into the artistic mentality of the Thracian ruling class, regardless of whether individual vessels were produced by local, Greek or Persian gold- and silversmiths. Vessels made during the acme of Thracian civilization, i.e. between the 6th and 3rd centuries B.C., offer a particularly grand multiplicity of form and decoration. Additionally, finds from both earlier and later periods testify to a long-lived tradition stretching from the Bronze Age right down to the era of Roman rule in Thrace.

Jewelry and Personal Ornaments

5

In addition to producing vessels to adorn the tables of kings and aristocrats or for use in ritual ceremonies, the Thracian goldsmiths also made personal and costume jewelry from precious metals. As in the case of silver and gold vessels, two of the primary concerns of Thracian craftsmen in manufacturing articles of jewelry were the use of precious metals and the predilection for the surface decoration of objects. However, it must be remembered that both vessels and jewelry made of precious metals were only available, in view of their high price, to members of a privileged social class. Thus the work of the goldsmiths represented primarily the artistic tastes of this numerically small stratum of the population.

The forms and decorative motifs of the individual items of jewelry again reflect foreign cultural influences. On the one hand one finds stylistic elements, figures and ornamentation borrowed from Achaemenid art, e.g. the zoomorphic motifs. On the other hand many items bear similarities to their counterparts in neighboring areas such as Macedonia and Thessaly. Technical developments in this craft came more slowly in Thrace than in adjacent regions. For example, the use of granulation for the decoration of jewelry can be traced back in Macedonia and Asia Minor at least to the 7th century B.C. whereas Thracian goldsmiths did not begin to make use of this technique until the late 6th century B.C. Nevertheless, on the whole the working of precious metals reached a very high level of development in Thrace. In the early 3rd century B.C. several workshops existed in the Greek coastal colony of Messambria (today Nessebur), whence the products found their way all over Thrace as well as abroad.

The excavation of a female burial from the second half of the 4th century B.C. in a necropolis near Metsek (in Haskovo district in south-eastern Bulgaria) yielded a collection of gold objects which includes examples of the main types of Thracian jewelry (pl. **29**). The necklace consists of a series of spherules with two conical terminals, all decorated with granulation, and a pendant, likewise adorned with granulation, in the form of a stylized vase. This form of chain and pendant was part of a tradition going back as far as the 6th century B.C. and is also characteristic of finds from Macedonia and Thessaly as well as those from Thrace. By contrast, the two similar pairs of earrings are a direct expression of the taste—the fashion—of the second half of the 4th century B.C. They reflect the archetypal form of Thracian earrings: an open ring thickened at one end. The thick end of the rings bears the stylized form of a lion's head, a feature which harks back to Persian traditions.

The personal jewelry is supplemented by costume jewelry. The four plaques, each decorated with a clearly defined symmetrical rosette, and the two irregularly shaped appliqués with their schematic plant motifs all have an eyelet at the back by which they were sewed onto the clothing.

In addition to the types of jewelry found in the vaulted tomb at Metsek it was also customary for both men and women in Thrace to wear a gold headpiece in the form of a diadem or wreath. Beside the female skeleton in the large grave mound at Vratsa dating from the second quarter of the 4th century B.C. a most naturalistic laurel wreath of gold foil was discovered (pl. **33**). The motif of the evergreen laurel was used way back in antiquity as a mark of honor for the services of a general, politician or even artist. The extremely lavish nature of the grave goods found under the Vratsa mound shows that two very important persons—a male skeleton was also found—were buried there.

Although it is known that the Celts came to Thrace in the 3rd century B.C. only a few scattered traces of archaeological evidence attesting this have been found. One very eloquent testimony to their presence, however, is the gold torque which was discovered in northwestern Bulgaria (pl. 31). To date only two examples of this typically Celtic form of necklace have been found on Thracian territory south of the Danube. Stylistically it is reminiscent of finds unearthed in Gaul. For the Celts the torque served not only as an item of jewelry but also as a mark of distinction or badge of rank. It is possible that the Thracians also employed it in this sense.

From the centuries following the Celtic invasion come two silver disks used for embellishing ceremonial armor (pl. 32). On one appears the bust of the so-called Great Goddess, who is wearing eight torques around her neck, while the other bears a picture of a horseman—the mounted Thracian Hero—who also has several torques.

These three or four items show the influence of Celtic art, which otherwise made hardly any inroads into the areas south of the Danube, whereas in the Dacian settlements between the Danube and the Carpathians Celtic influence, both in the development of art and in other fields, is clearly apparent.

Thracian finds have produced earrings in great quantity and diversity. Among the earliest finds of Thracian jewelry adorned with granulation are the ten identical earrings from the oldest grave mound in the necropolis near Douvanli, which has been dated to the second half of the 6th century B.C. (pl. 37). The thick ends of the open rings are decorated with various geometrical patterns of gold globules. Originally the thicker end of the ring, which served to allow it to hang properly, was not decorated, but gradually it developed into an object of decoration in its own right. Goldsmiths frequently made use of geometrical forms, such as can be seen from the gold earring found at Boyana near Sofia (pl. 30). It is a pyramid design terminating in two spherules, and the three facades are beset with granulation. A pendant which was also found at Boyana had exactly the same form and decoration. Evidently, the two pieces once formed part of the same set.

The heavy end of an earring was sometimes given the form of an animal's head or a fantastic creature, like the one from the vaulted tomb at Metsek, or—though more rarely—of a human mask. The gold earrings in the form of a maenad's head (pl. 35) were made in the 3rd century B.C. in a workshop at Messambria. Both the subject matter—in Greek mythology the maenads were the female companions of the wine-god Dionysus—and the style show Greek influence. This is hardly surprising when one considers that this old Thracian coastal settlement enjoyed a big economic boost following the establishment of a Greek colony there.

Another product of the workshops at Messambria in the early 3rd century B.C. was a pair of earrings with a winged-horse *protome*, representing the figure of Pegasus from Greek mythology, and pendants in the form of miniature amphorae decorated with granulation (pl. 34).

From the same grave mound which contained the gold laurel wreath and gold jar depicting the quadrigae (see above) comes the exquisite pair of earrings shown in plate 36. They consist of two richly decorated disks to which a lunate pendant is attached via a link in the form of a winged sphinx. Hanging from each crescent are five delicate gold chains with acorn pendants. Similar earrings were in vogue at this time in Macedonia.

The few bracelets which have been discovered in Thracian finds have a plainer design than contemporary earrings and necklaces. The two bangles of twisted gold wire shown in plate 64 were found near Skrebatno on the south-eastern slope of the Pirin mountains. On both the ends of the open rings become wider. In one case they form flat triangular surfaces with dotted ornaments and in the other double volutes. They were made by local goldsmiths in the 5th century B.C.

Thracian finger-rings often bear figurative reliefs. The subject was often a deity or the Thracian Horseman, though this does not necessarily indicate that such rings were an integral part of the ceremonial rituals, e.g. part of the priest's garb. Most rings which have

Preceding page

29 Collection of gold jewelry from the vaulted tomb near Metsek (Cat. No. 1.11.1)

30 Gold earring from Boyana (Cat. No. 3.10)
31 Gold torque from Cibur Varosh (Cat. No. 3.9)

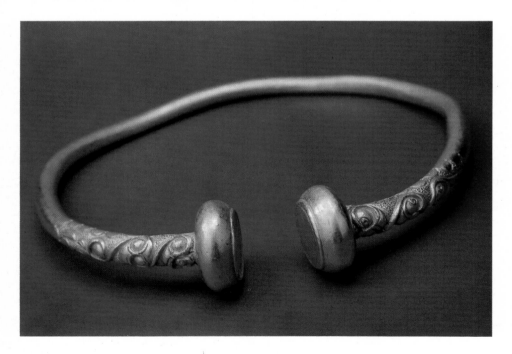

32 Parcel-gilt silver ornaments from Galiche (Cat. No. 2.11)

33 Gold laurel wreath
from the grave mound at
Vratsa (Cat. No. 1.10.5)

34 Gold earrings from the necropolis of Messambria (Cat. No. 1.14.2)

35 Gold earring from the necropolis of Messambria (Cat. No. 1.14.1)

36 Gold earrings from the grave mound at Vratsa (Cat. No. 1.10.6)
37 Gold earrings from a barrow near Douvanli (Cat. No. 1.3.2)

38 Gold finger-rings
from the 4th century B.C.
(Cat. No. 3.12)

39 Spiral gold finger-ring from the necropolis of Messambria (Cat. No. 1.14.4)
40 Spiral gold ring from the necropolis of Messambria (Cat. No. 1.14.3)

41 Gold pectoral from a barrow near Douvanli (Cat. No. 1.3.5)
42 Gold pectoral from a barrow near Staro Selo (Cat. No. 1.4)

43 Iron pectoral coated with gilt silver from the vaulted tomb near Metsek (Cat. No. 1.11.2)

44 Gold pectoral from
a barrow near Douvanli
(Cat. No. 1.3.3)

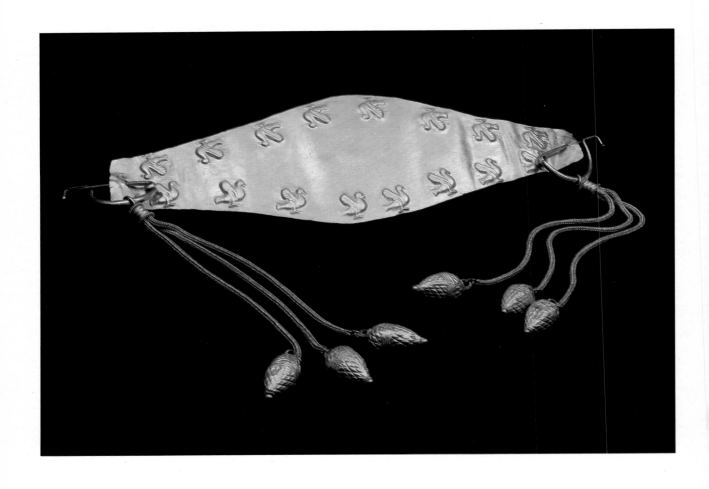

45   Gold jewelry from
the hoard of Nikolayevo
(Cat. No. 2.14)

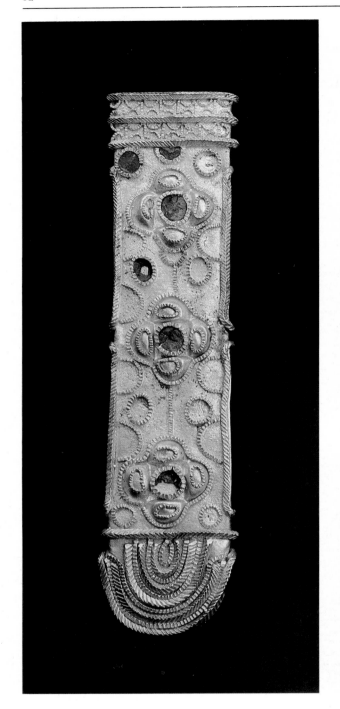

46   Gold fitting for a dagger sheath, gold with gemstone inlays (Cat. No. 3.3)
47   Bronze halter ring from the vaulted tomb near Metsek (Cat. No. 1.11.3)
48   Stone mold for a bronze scepter mount from Pobit Kamuk (Cat. No. 2.1)

49   Parcel-gilt silver bust of Heracles on a bronze chariot fitting from Shishkovtsi (Cat. No. 1.18)

51 Bronze suit of armor from a barrow near Ruets (Cat. No. 1.7)

53 Ceremonial bronze helmet with frieze of gods from a barrow near Bryastovets (Cat. No. 1.15)

54 Ceremonial iron helmet with silver face mask from a barrow in Plovdiv (Cat. No. 1.16)

55 Ceremonial iron helmet with face mask of bronze partly coated with silver found in a grave mound near Chatalka (Cat. No. 1.17)

56 Parcel-gilt silver greave from the grave mound at Vratsa (Cat. No. 1.10.7)

57 Gilt relief on the greave from Vratsa (Cat. No. 1.10.7)

58 Silver shield plaque from a grave mound near Panagyurishte (Cat. No. 1.12.1)

59 Silver shield plaque from a grave mound near Panagyurishte (Cat. No. 1.12.2)

60 Marble votive relief
for the Thracian Horseman
from Kaspichan
(Cat. No. 3.16)

61 Bronze statuettes depicting the Thracian Horseman (Cat. No. 3.15)

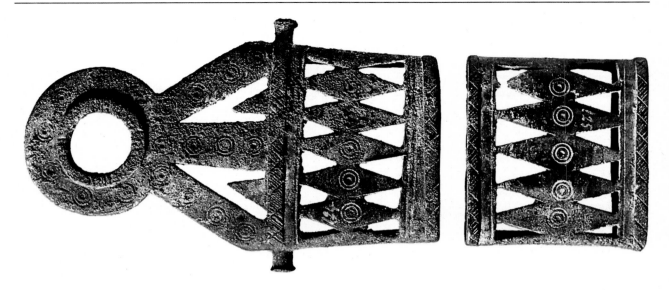

62 Bronze belt clasp and fitting with geometric decoration from Vidin (Cat. No. 3.4)
63 Gold belt fitting with figurative relief from Lovets (Cat. No. 3.13)

been found in Thrace were made in local workshops. Their decorative designs show up an artistic idiosyncrasy which we also noted in the case of the gold jar from Vratsa: whereas the horses are portrayed in a fairly convincing and naturalistic manner, the depiction of people is somewhat clumsy. This can be seen, for example, on a gold ring dating from the 4th century B.C. (pl. **38**, right). Despite the strong element of stylization the anatomical details of the horse (with the exception of the forelegs) are largely correct, but the figure of the man is grossly distorted. Another ring (pl. **38**, left) gives a more accurate representation of a horse and rider in motion. The horse is galloping forward and the rider's chlamys is fluttering behind him. He has a pointed beard, and both he and his mount have been depicted clearly and in their proper proportions.

Rings sometimes bear stylized zoomorphic designs. Two spiralled rings with animal motifs were found at Nessebur, products of a goldsmith's workshop there of the 3rd century B.C. The two ends of one ring portray the head and tail of a dragon (pl. **39**) whose body and tail were once beset with precious gems—one amethyst still remains embedded in the beast's back—while the other has the form of a snake (pl. **40**).

One of the characteristic forms of personal ornament in Thrace was the pectoral, a decorated plate worn on the breast which was either fastened to the clothing through clasps (fibulae) or sewn on. These ornamental plates, the upper edge of which normally lay level with the collar bone, were extremely popular in the ancient Oriental civilizations, and a number have been found in areas where the Mycenaean culture had spread. The Thracians probably adopted the custom of wearing pectorals from their eastern neighbors. To date more than 30 pectorals from Thrace have come to light, of which the majority were found in what is today southern Bulgaria, while only four examples have been discovered between the Balkan mountains and the Danube. North of the Danube, in Dacian territory, such chest ornaments do not appear to have been worn.

A gold pectoral from a grave mound in the necropolis at Douvanli dating from the middle of the 5th century B.C. clearly shows the links with the eastern cultures (pl. **41**). The half-moon plate bears the stylized design

64 Gold bangles from Skrebatno (Cat. No. 3.7)

65   Silver breastplate from a barrow near Boukyovtsi
(Cat. No. 1.5.2)

of a lion, which is reminiscent of depictions of animals in Iranian art. At the sides of the pectoral there are small holes for attaching it to the clothing.

A different example of this kind of decorative ornament was likewise found in the necropolis at Douvanli in one of the oldest and most sumptuously decorated tombs in the cemetery (pl. **44**). Persian influence is again apparent in the bird designs which line the periphery of this rhombic pectoral of gold foil made in the late 6th century B.C., at a time when the Persian king Darius had extended his sway as far as the Balkan peninsula. However, alongside the Persian stylistic elements there are also clearly discernible indigenous Thracian forms such as the two fibulae at the sides which served to attach the plate to the clothing. The motif of the two sets of three chains with acorn pendants reoccurs on other items of jewelry and ornaments produced in Thrace and was a popular theme among the Thracians over a long period.

Around the edge of an elliptical pectoral of gold foil, likewise from southern Bulgaria and dating from the second quarter of the 5th century B.C. (pl. **42**), is a frieze of lotus blossoms alternating with hook-shaped ornaments. The latter motif is also found on Thracian earrings and thus shows this pectoral to be the product of a Thracian workshop. In the center is a geometrical pattern: a heavily stylized version of the Tree of Life, which was a commonly depicted theme in Achaemenid art. This pectoral is thus an amalgam of various artistic traditions welded together to form a new composition —this indeed was the epitome of Thracian art.

An unusual and late example of a pectoral was found in the vaulted tomb near Metsek dating from the second half of the 4th century B.C. (pl. **43**). The crescent-shaped ornamental breastplate consists of an iron base coated with a thin sheet of silver. It is decorated with several ornamental bands depicting geometric and vegetable designs as well as female and lion masks. The plate was part of a ceremonial suit of iron armor in which the deceased was buried.

A different kind of silver breastplate was unearthed in a find in north-western Bulgaria from the 4th century B.C. (pl. **65**). It is made up of six oddly shaped fibulae linked by chains to a central rosette. From the fibulae

hang more rosettes and human masks to which in turn are attached more chains with pendants in the form of acorns and poppy seeds. The rosettes, with their star and floral forms, can be recognized as traditional Thracian motifs, and the execution of the human faces again betrays the same clumsiness that was apparent in the depiction of people on the gold rings and on the jar from the Vratsa mound. This is another indication that this pectoral was the work of a Thracian silversmith.

Even during the centuries of foreign domination, when independent national artistic development was no longer possible, there were still plenty of craftsmen and workshops in Thrace. Indeed, the influence of the Romans in the provinces of Lower Moesia (broadly equivalent to northern Bulgaria between the Danube and the Balkan mountains) and Thrace (today southern Bulgaria and the adjoining area) even led to a big upsurge in municipal culture in which handicrafts played a major role. The products of Roman craftsmanship began to exert an increasingly dominant influence and largely dictated the tastes of the Romanized population, particularly in the towns. Local craftsmen adopted Roman production techniques and imitated Roman forms with the result that indigenous artistic traditions in Thrace, as in most provinces throughout the Roman empire, were largely abandoned.

This same process was reflected in the products of the goldsmith's trade. Thus the individual components of the collection of gold jewelry shown in plate **45** no longer bear the traces of Thracian artistic traditions. A new feature of the work of Thracian goldsmiths was the frequent use of precious and semi-precious stones. For example, for the chain pendant illustrated a gold coin bearing the portrait of the Roman emperor Caracalla (A.D. 211 to 217) was chosen and framed by a gem-studded border. The coin enables us to date the whole collection to the first half of the 3rd century A.D. It was a flourishing period in the life of the Roman provinces on the Balkan peninsula, a time when economic developments had reached a peak. The jewelry collection from Nikolayevo reflects the wealth of the leading social stratum in the towns, a stratum drawn from various national groups which, in the process of Romanization, fused together to form a new ruling class.

6

Thracian Armor, Weapons and the Cult of the Thracian Horseman

Among friend and foe alike the Thracians were renowned as courageous fighters. Homer highlighted their martial virtues in the *Iliad*. When Odysseus and his companions killed many of the Thracians, who were fighting on the side of the Trojans, during a night raid they were dazzled by the magnificence of their weapons, by the richly adorned armor and their war chariots, and they gleefully took the exceptionally beautiful and swift horses back to the Greek camp as booty.

However, in the centuries following the composition of the Homeric epics the Thracian military strategy altered, and the armies of the Odrysian kings were overwhelmingly made up of warriors on horseback. In Roman documents, too, the Thracians appear as mounted cavalry units whose leaders rode into battle in a light, two-wheeled chariot. Many brave and sturdy Thracians were taken off by the Romans to Italy where they were trained as gladiators and then sent out into the arena for exhibition fights.

War played a dominant role in the lives of the Thracians, as indeed it did for all the nations of antiquity. This fact is naturally reflected in the archaeological finds which, fortunately, thus supplement the rather generalized information provided by the written records, thereby giving us a detailed picture of the weaponry and armor of the time. Unfortunately, the further we go back in history, the scarcer become both the written references and the material deposits which would enable us to deepen our knowledge of the lives of the various peoples in times both of peace and of war.

Nevertheless, it is frequently possible to apply insights gained from later finds to earlier periods. Homer, for instance, mentions that the Thracians used war chariots with metal fittings, but the only archaeological evidence for such chariots so far found in burial sites comes from a much later period. In a grave mound near Metsek, Haskovo district, some solid bronze rings were found which were decorated at the top with heavily stylized human masks (pl. **47**) and which were used for fastening and guiding a horse's halter. Such metal elements fixed to the wooden chariots—which were actually used in battle—originally served to make the vehicle more stable while at the same time providing additional protection against the attacks of the enemy. Ceremonial chariots were also made for victory parades or for funeral rituals, and though they resembled the real war chariots their metal fittings were geared more towards ostentation rather than protection. An example of such extravagant metal ornamentation on a chariot from Roman times (2nd to 3rd century A.D.) was found in western Bulgaria. It included a hexagonal bronze plate decorated with a parcel-gilt silver bust of the Greek demigod Heracles (pl. **49**). Heracles was famed for his feats of heroism, and his portrayal on various pieces of Thracian armor was intended both to protect the wearer and to serve as a model of valor.

After it was discovered how to produce and alloy bronze and to work it through the technique of casting, it became possible to manufacture much more effective weapons. In addition to the short, straight dagger the main weapon used by the Thracians from the Bronze Age onwards was the sword. Its form resembled in many respects that of the swords used in the late Bronze Age culture of the neighboring Mycenaean empire (approximately the third quarter of the 2nd millennium B.C.—pl. **66**, second from the right), and it also bore a

66 Late Bronze Age weapons from various Thracian finds (Cat. No. 3.2)

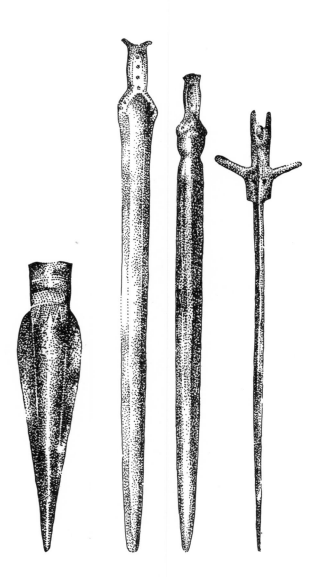

resemblance to that used by the Thracians' northern neighbors in the Carpathian basin (pl. **66**, second from the left and right).

Swords and daggers were kept in sheaths of wood or leather, which were reinforced with a metal strip; some sheaths were made of more precious materials and were richly adorned. At Belogradets, Varna district, a dagger sheath was found fitted with soldered gold wire trimmings and amber inlays (pl. **46**). It represents one of the few extant products of the goldsmith's art from the 8th/7th centuries B.C., a rather shadowy period as far as our knowledge of the political, social and cultural developments of the Thracians is concerned, which was ended by the foundation of Greek colonies in the coastal regions.

In addition to sword and dagger, the lance was also widely used by the Thracians in battle. The wooden shaft was capped by a bronze tip (pl. **66**, left).

Swords, daggers, lance tips as well as objects of a more peaceful nature such as scepter mounts, hatchets or ceremonial axes were manufactured according to the same technique of bronze-casting using a stone mold with one or two sections. Several such molds have been found in Thracian areas. They show the negative form of the relevant cast—plate **48** shows a mold for a spiral scepter mount—plus individual pouring channels. Such molds had to be very carefully made and represented for their owners objects of considerable value. This is the only possible explanation for the fact that, at a site in northern Bulgaria, five stone molds were discovered which had evidently been hurriedly buried in a moment of danger as very valuable objects. This chance find has also proved most valuable to the archaeologists of today in view of their scientific importance, since they provide us on the one hand with more detailed information concerning the production techniques used for casting, and on the other testify to their great material value in the society of the time.

The finds from Thrace contain more examples of armor than of weaponry. The types of armor found again indicate that they were intended for mounted warriors. The main element in the rider's defensive array was the breastplate made of bronze or iron. Two basic forms existed. The first was a bell-shaped cuirass which the

Thracians developed from Greek prototypes; it broadened out below the waist to allow the rider more manœuvrability. The other type of breastplate ended at the waist where it was joined by rings or hinges to other metal plates for the protection of the lower body (pl. **51**). A typical feature of these breastplates of sheet metal was the schematic depiction of chest muscles and the lower ribs. Sometimes these lines were worked up into decorative motifs which in some cases even took the form of snakes or dragons, a stylistic device again borrowed from eastern traditions.

From the 4th century B.C. onwards the solid breastplate increasingly gave way to a lighter and more mobile leather tunic with metal fittings. These fittings provided an opportunity for decoration with ornaments or even figures, and a new type of ornament arose: the *phalera*. The *phalerae* were normally round and were attached to the underlying surface by means of small rivets. They bore designs in low relief ranging from simple rosette patterns to complex figurative scenes. The favorite figures for depiction were deities or heroes, so that the *phalera* became something of an amulet, to protect its wearer from danger or harm. As indicated above, the Greek hero Heracles was credited with particular power in this respect. Examples of the *phalera* include the two items from pre-Roman times already described (pl. **32**) decorated with the bust of the Great Goddess and a depiction of the Thracian Horseman.

Whereas finds of armor in Thrace have been spread fairly evenly both to the south and north of the Balkan mountains, finds of another important item of defensive equipment—the helmet—have occurred mainly in the south. Helmets were usually cast or forged from bronze and had a variety of forms. Either they covered the whole head, in which case small apertures were made for the eyes, ears, nose and mouth (pl. **50**), or else they covered only the upper part of the head and had cheek-flaps which were either fixed or hinged to the base of the helmet. Yet another kind of bronze helmet ended in a pointed tip in imitation of a soft felt hat—the so-called Phrygian cap (pl. **67**). In terms of the level of the productive forces in the 5th to 4th century B.C. these helmets were all mass-produced articles, and so considerations of artistic decoration played only a minor role.

67 Bronze helmet in the form of a Phrygian cap from Gurmen (Cat. No. 3.14)

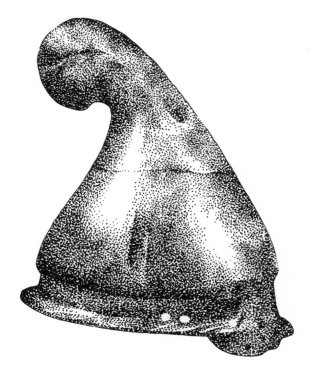

68 Ceremonial silver helmet with gilt reliefs from the grave mound near Agighiol (Cat. No. 1.6.1)

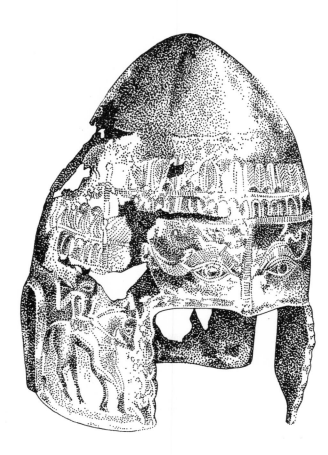

In addition there were also decorated helmets of varying degrees of ornateness which it is hard to imagine were ever worn in a real battle. Plate **52** shows an example of a decorated bronze helmet from the second half of the 5th century B.C. which is closely based on the real battle helmet, differing only in its sparse ornamentation. Around the rim is an ornamental frieze punctuated by a palmette in the center. Beneath the palmette the nasal can still be seen, though the cheek-flaps, which were once attached to the helmet by hinges, are now missing. Two symmetrically confronted griffins adorn the crown of the helmet.

A parcel-gilt silver helmet found in a prince's grave near Agighiol (in Tulcea district in Romania) dating from the 4th century B.C. is richly decorated with ornamental and figurative reliefs (pl. **68**). It lay among other items of weaponry and armor, decorative horse bridle trappings and several *phialai*. Two eyes are depicted on the front of the helmet which, in accordance with the prevailing religious and mythological notions of the time, had an apotropaic purpose. The same function of warding off evil was probably served by the relief on the cheek-flap showing an armored horseman brandishing a lance in his right hand—another depiction of the Thracian Horseman. The crown of the helmet is decorated with bands of tongues and palms.

On the Black Sea coast south of the Balkan mountains a bronze helmet dating from Roman times was found (pl. **53**). It has a simple form with a pointed peak and originally had two hinged cheek-flaps. The frieze around the crown shows a series of gods within an arcaded framework portraying Apollo, Minerva, Nike, Mars and Mercury while Neptune appears on the one remaining cheek-flap. The decorative motif—all the deities depicted are drawn from the Graeco-Roman mythological tradition—, the form and the style of this ornate helmet all reflect the strong Roman influence on Thracian craftsmanship in the first few centuries A.D. The craftsman who made this helmet was possibly himself a Roman.

Another variety of ceremonial helmet was the mask-helmet, which also dates from the time of the Roman empire. These helmets carried a facial mask after the fashion of Roman sculptures, so that each helmet became an individual work of art. The Romans made use of such masks for the cult of ancestor worship. At a burial, for example, masks portraying the forefathers of the deceased would be carried along during the funeral procession. Another component of Roman burial customs were funeral games held in honor of the deceased. Such games and also death-masks were part of the funeral rites of many other peoples in the Mediterranean area and had a long tradition. Although it cannot be demonstrated with certainty that the Thracian helmet-mask from Roman times was one of the many cultural variations on the theme of ancestor worship and funeral games, it is nevertheless highly probable that its function and significance are to be explained in these terms.

Stylistically the helmet-masks relate to Roman portrait art in many ways, though occasionally local peculiarities come more to the forefront.

A helmet-mask found near a Roman villa in southern Bulgaria has a calotte of iron while the face is of bronze foil and was originally coated with silver (pl. 55). Just above the hairline is a hinge connecting the two separate parts of the mask together. The face is that of a young man with uniform features and meticulously curled hair, which is reminiscent of the hairstyle occurring in Roman portraits from the first half of the 1st century A.D. The eyes, nostrils and mouth all have openings so that the helmet could actually be used.

Another helmet-mask found in southern Bulgaria, at Plovdiv, has an upper part of iron while the face and laurel wreath are of silver foil (pl. 54). On the forehead, hidden by the hairline, and behind the ears are connecting hinges and hooks. Although stylistically this mask is basically similar to the one discussed above and can thus be presumed to date from roughly the same period, there are nevertheless clear differences in the facial features and in the artistic execution. These can perhaps be explained by the fact that in the design of the silver mask from Plovdiv local artistic traditions were more prevalent while the craftsman responsible for the other mask adhered more closely to the contemporary urban Roman archetype.

Another element of Thracian armor was the greave, which was indispensable in mounted warfare. In general greaves were made of bronze foil and reproduced the

69 Parcel-gilt silver greaves from the grave mound near Agighiol (Cat. No. 1.6.2)

shape of the human shinbone and knee. There were also some magnificently decorated greaves of which the one from Vratsa is a prime example (pl. **56**). It is made of parcel-gilt silver foil and depicts a goddess. The knee-guard forms her head while other parts of her body, such as the arms and legs, are represented in very abstract form as snakes with fantastic heads (pl. **57**). On her forehead she wears a wreath of ivy. The right side of her face is covered with horizontal gold stripes, which should be seen as indicating a tattoo. Certain tattoos were worn as marks of distinction by aristocratic Thracian women or priestesses, and they were also a sign of divinity.

The custom of decorating greaves with a female mask to bestow an apotropaic power on them was taken over by the Thracians from the Greeks, among whom this function was performed by Gorgon heads. However, the Thracian craftsmen altered the Greek original and substituted for the Gorgon heads new totems drawn from their own mythology together with stylistic elements taken from Persian-Achaemenid art.

The greave was found in the same grave mound from the second quarter of the 4th century B.C. as the gold jar with the two quadrigae, the laurel wreath of gold foil and the exquisite pair of earrings; but no other items of armor or weaponry were found, for it was the grave of a woman. In this case, therefore, the greave should not be construed as having its original protective function. The fact that it portrays the Great Mother-Goddess elevates it above its original role and bestows on it instead a more general function as an amulet for the protection of the wearer against all harm and evil.

In another magnificently furnished grave at Agighiol in Romania a pair of similar greaves were found (pl. **69**). The knee section of one of them depicts, like the one from Vratsa, a woman's face decorated with stripes of gold foil and a body composed of snakes. On the other the face is not tattooed and the calf section bears a relief of a mounted warrior, a majestic figure and a fantastic monster. Alongside the man who was laid in this grave were buried, in addition to the richly adorned helmet described above (pl. **68**), arrowheads, slingshot stones, appliqués for armor and horse harness as well as several silver and bronze *phialai*. Thus, in contrast to the single greave found in the female burial at Vratsa, the pair of greaves from Agighiol formed part of the ceremonial armor of the deceased.

Belts, sometimes decorated with metal trimmings, completed the defensive outfit of the Thracian warrior. In north-western Bulgaria a bronze buckle plus another metal fitting from the same belt were discovered (pl. **62**). They are rare examples of finds dating from the "dark age" of Thrace before the foundation of the Greek towns in this region, and illustrate the strictly geometrical art which characterizes objects from the 8th to 7th century B.C. The predominance of geometrical designs and the almost total absence of figurative motifs was also typical of Greek art at this time and testifies to Thrace's close incorporation into the general line of cultural development in the eastern Mediterranean during this era.

We may compare this with a metal belt fitting of gilt silver foil made in the 5th to 4th century B.C. (pl. **63**). Little silver nails secured it to a leather belt. The scene depicted in relief on the metal plaque is typical of the period and shows an archer, a horseman and several animals symmetrically grouped around a stylized Tree of Life. A comparison of the two belt fittings indicates the progress made by Thracian craftsmanship between the 8th and the 4th centuries B.C. from simple geometric forms to the free representation of figures and scenes.

Thracian shields were, in accordance with their function of providing protection for the mounted soldiers, relatively small and light. They were made of wood or leather reinforced by metal nails or metal plates. On shields which formed part of a suit of ceremonial armor and which thus were possibly never worn in a real battle, these plates were frequently decorated with ornaments or figures. However, such decorative elements on Thracian shields were not identification signs, as they were in medieval Europe. They basically portrayed the same motifs and were based on the same artistic premises as the decoration on other pieces of Thracian armor and weaponry.

From the same find come two stylistically different silver shield plaques. The larger decorative plate is rectangular and has a rosette as its central motif (pl. **58**) on either side of which is a winged imaginary beast. At the bottom is a siren and at the top Heracles subduing the Nemean lion. Originally this plate decorated the middle of a shield and was surrounded by a series of round plates with a convex center around which were more ornaments; the one illustrated shows two confronted animals separated by a palmette, and opposite this a bird (pl. **59**).

The decoration, which was at times extremely ornate, on the military equipment of the mounted warriors reflected the high esteem in which the latter were held. This elevated position of the horseman was also reflected in Thracian religion, though our knowledge of this is very vague owing to the lack of written records. In the works of Greek authors there are very few references to this aspect of the lives of their neighbors, for Thracian religious ideas were alien to the Greeks who, as a result, took so little trouble to find out about them that the information they have bequeathed to us in this respect is very sketchy.

Nevertheless, we do know from archaeological finds that the horseman figure also played a central role in Thracian cult worship. Monuments to the Thracian Horseman, who appears to have been a nameless god, have only existed since the Hellenistic age when Thrace was under Macedonian rule. Stylistically they are closely related to the Greek depictions of horsemen from the 4th century B.C., though the majority of the consecrated reliefs and votive figures dedicated to the Thracian Horseman were not produced until the time of the Roman empire.

The standard presentation of the Thracian Horseman shows him in profile on a cantering or galloping horse. In his right hand he brandishes a lance and his chlamys streams out behind him. This is the depiction, for example, which we find in a bronze statuette from Roman times (pl. **61**, left) which also highlights the horse's richly adorned bridle and the rider's decorated armor. The other statuette depicted in plate **61** shows the demigod in a less belligerent pose, holding an offering bowl in his right hand.

The Thracian Horseman, who was a half human, half divine figure, was invoked by people in various situations in life to provide help and support. From the varying choice of attributes or from the naming of

Greek or Latin deities on the frame of the relief it is possible to ascertain which of his properties or abilities the donor wished to invoke. Thus one sacred marble relief dedicated to the mounted Hero (pl. **60**) shows him as a middle-aged man with curly hair and beard redolent of the portrayal of Greek gods. In his right hand he is holding a cornucopia, dispensing benediction and prosperity.

This shows that the Thracian Horseman was seen as a fertility god. The posture of both rider and horse clearly indicates that this relief, unlike the two statuettes, was not intended to present the actual motion of the horse but rather to serve as a cult figure for the purpose of veneration, since the horse's gallop is frozen into a symbolic pose with its right foreleg on a little round altar. Beneath the horse two smaller animals are locked in struggle, but only a few key details are sketched—just enough for the comprehension of the scene illustrated.

A dog, which was often depicted accompanying the Thracian Horseman, is biting the snout of a boar. This scene, too, had a significance of its own within the overall framework of the relief, yet today it is equally as incomprehensible to us as many other aspects of the cult of the Thracian Horseman, since the knowledge we have gleaned from pictorial representations has not been supplemented by written records.

We have already referred at various points to the high regard which the Thracians had for their horses. This was principally due to the horse's great importance in battle, both as a draft animal for pulling chariots and as a mount for the cavalryman. Just as the king, the generals and outstanding warriors had sumptuously decorated ceremonial armor and equipment, so the harnesses of their horses were also richly adorned. Homer, for example, mentions this in his accounts. Pictorial representations made by the Thracians themselves —such as the equine *rhyton* from Douvanli (pl. **24**), the gold jar from Vratsa (pl. **19**) and the bronze statuettes (pl. **61**)—show that the decoration of the horses was concentrated on the straps around the head and hocks.

When a king or member of the ruling class died, assuming he had earned military honors during his lifetime, it was the custom among the Thracians to bury him not only with his ceremonial armor but with his horses and war chariot as well. Whereas the horses which were teamed up to the chariot—itself bearing decorative fittings—wore largely plain harnesses, the chargers were adorned with numerous decorative plaques of valuable metals. Ornate bridles and harnesses are especially common in graves dating from the second half of the 5th century B.C., a time when the Odrysian kings had consolidated their rule and had extended their sway over large stretches of the Balkan peninsula. Their power rested on an army which was largely made up of cavalry units.

However, individual examples of metal embellishments for horse harnesses made by Thracian craftsmen also exist from earlier times. Among these is a decorative bronze plate with molded mountings which was found in north-western Bulgaria (pl. **72**). It was fastened to the horse's forehead by means of a strap. Geometric patterns have been engraved on the outer part of the elliptical plate. At the sides and at the bottom is a double volute, while two stylized wings as well as the tail of a bird appear at the top end. Below them is a protuberant boss into which geometric patterns have been etched. On the opposite narrow end is a three-dimensional animal head—its horns, eyes and snout are all discernible. This decorative plate, which was made in the 7th century B.C., is characterized by the reduction of all the ornamentation to basic geometric shapes such as circles, triangles, spirals etc. On the other hand, the inclusion of the odd element of figurative decoration suggests that this bridle frontlet stems from the later phase of geometric art in Thrace.

To an ever increasing extent figurative designs displaced the geometrical patterns, as we can see from the silver brow-piece found in a grave mound dating from *c*. 400 B.C. (pl. **77**). Here the underlying elliptical form is barely recognizable; the decoration consists of a sculptured lion's head above the guide runner and a second, flat lion mask without the lower jaw. Only in very rare cases were human masks depicted rather than animal heads.

Such metal bases with heads affixed were used to decorate horse harnesses down the ages. Other metal bridle trappings were worked only in low relief. In general such fittings were fastened to the straps in pairs, and the decoration consisted in most cases of animal motifs. This clear preference for zoomorphic designs rather than vegetable ornaments or human figures was not a phenomenon restricted to Thracian art; it has been giv-

70 Two bridle trappings in the form of the forequarters of a lion from a grave mound near Panagyurishte (Cat. No. 1.12.3)

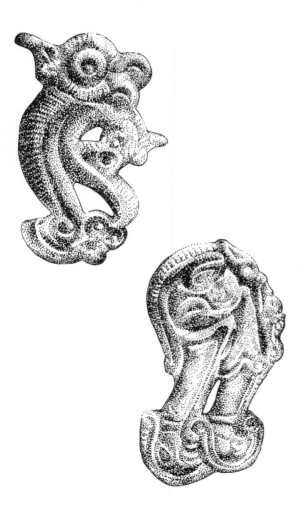

en the generic term Animal Style. The Animal Style first emerged around the 7th century B.C. among nomadic peoples living on the steppes of Eurasia who lived largely by hunting and raising cattle. It was thus understandable that animals also figured prominently in their religious notions and cult ceremonies. These groups also worshipped animals as tribal totems.

As a result of the frequent population shifts which occurred in these areas some nomadic tribes came into contact with Iranian art, in which the depiction of animals and fantastic creatures was very popular. The fusion of their animal motifs with stylistic themes taken from Iranian art led to the birth of a new art-form which was specific to the nomadic peoples and which was characterized by the Animal Style. Tribal migrations resulted in the spreading of these artistic ideas, including to the Black Sea and the eastern Mediterranean, where the Scythians and the Thracians were especially influenced by the Animal Style.

Much discussion has gone on about whether the Thracians adopted the Animal Style from the Scythians or, conversely, whether the Scythians borrowed the idea from the Thracians. Clearly there were artistic contacts between the two neighboring nations, but the question of the predominance of the one or the other is superfluous, since the Animal Style of both nations emerged from common roots before developing in accordance with the social conditions prevailing in their respective territories.

In the art of those nations such as the Thracians and the Scythians who had become sedentary the Animal Style took on a new meaning. Among these peoples socio-economic developments had already led to the formation of a tribal aristocracy and to the emergence of a nation-state. Under these social conditions the Animal Style became associated with the art of the ruling elite and became the bearer of its ideology. Thus scenes showing animals locked in struggle, for example, were no longer depicted for their own sake or to conjure up the magic of the chase, they were now also symbols of the struggle for real power within society. Lions and griffins became marks of regal might, and animal motifs were also employed to express the cult notions of the rulers.

In portraying the Animal Style most artists were not concerned with achieving a naturalistic representation. The natural forms were in fact stylized to such an extent that only token signs remained which, however, strongly emphasized certain basic features of the particular animal or fabulous monster. Thus the griffin, which was a common motif, was frequently portrayed merely as a head seen in profile, yet it was clearly identifiable as a griffin because of its sharply hooked and usually open beak and the large round eye (pl. **73**).

The schematic depiction of animals, reduced to the bare essentials, was fused into a geometric decorative scheme, thereby departing even more from the actual living form. A silver bridle plate from the Mogilanska mound at Vratsa, for example, depicts several animals framed by two lion tails with scroll terminals, the frame being punctured in just two places by a horse's ear and a bird's head (pl. **74**). A four-legged reptile-like creature crouches below the upper part of the frame, while only the heads of the other three animals—very generalized portrayals of a griffin, a horse and a bird—are visible. Once again the eyes are very prominent, and the manes, like the enclosing tails, are striated and terminate in a volute.

The artistic aim which the craftsmen using the Animal Style sought to achieve—the creation of decorative elements by means of animal motifs—could also be achieved by using other parts of the body which were not as characteristic of the animal as its head. An example of this is the silver appliqué illustrated in plate **75** which shows the forequarters of a lion. The various anatomical features depicted, such as the hide, the claws and the muscles, are heavily stylized and have a largely ornamental character.

This artistic principle is even more clearly visible in the case of two silver decorative trappings from the first half of the 4th century B.C. which were found in the Panagyurishte mound (pl. **70**). Once again the forequarters of a lion are depicted, but in this instance the ornamental lines based on anatomical features which we saw in the previous illustration have been supplanted by separate depictions of griffin heads which fill out the shoulder and both claws (pl. **70**, right). In the case of the adjacent appliqué (pl. **70**, left), the craftsman has taken the dissolution of the basic form even further: the outline of shoulder and forelegs is completely obscured by several ornamentally interlaced animal masks, so that the underlying form can only be perceived by analogy with the other ornament.

Some of the many variations on the theme of the Animal Style were brought to light by the find of some parcel-gilt bridle appliqués of silver which were unearthed together with three silver jars and nine *phialai* (including the one shown in plate **12**) as well as other metal objects. Made in the second half of the 4th century B.C., they were buried between 280 and 270 B.C. in the northern forelands of the Balkan mountains at a time when Thrace was being overrun by Celts from the north. This treasure was then rediscovered by chance in 1953 near the village of Loukovit, Lovech district. It contained a parcel-gilt silver brow-piece for a horse (pl. **78**) which bears the usual elliptical form. Around the edge is a decorative frill reminiscent of a lion's mane and in the center stands a three-dimensional griffin's head—for once with a closed beak—framed by two half-moon pectorals.

Two more decorative plates, which form a strictly symmetrical mirror-image of one another, portray a pair of recumbent winged lion-griffins (pl. **76**). The hind quarters of the two creatures are connected via a stylized bird's tail.

The incorporation of animal motifs into the overall pattern of ornamentation is particularly evident in the case of the three or four-vaned symbol which is frequently met with. In its basic form the four-vaned sign derives from the swastika, an old Indo-European sun symbol. It is undoubtedly no coincidence that this motif crops up commonly on horse trimmings, for to the Thracians the horse was not just important as a draft animal and a means of conveyance, it was also the sacred beast of the sun-god. Thus in venerating it the Thracians closely combined mythological ideas with experiences from everyday life. Among the items in the treasure of Loukovit are four appliqués in the form of a swastika consisting of four lion-griffins symmetrically grouped around an umbo (pl. **82**). Yet again the artist restricted himself to the representation of what he considered to be the essential features—the eye, ear, open mouth and mane—and through the juxtaposition of the stylized heads created a strictly ornamental design.

Rosettes blended into such a swastika composition more easily than animal representations, as two more plaques from Loukovit show (pl. **83**). In this instance the severity of the overall design is somewhat softened by the addition of scroll reliefs and the asymmetrical umbo. It also gives us some indication of the breadth of variety which was possible in respect of the Animal Style, which was not confined exclusively to animal motifs.

Although a characteristic feature of the Animal Style was its ornamental treatment of natural forms, there were also some examples of naturalistic portrayals of animals and occasionally even of people in connection with animals. Among this group are two decorative plates from Loukovit, each of which depicts a horseman fighting a lion (pl. **84**). Despite all the dynamism of the scene, which is expressed by the motion of the horse, the rider's flowing cloak and the contorted body of the lion, the contours of the work again show the ornamental regimentation of form which was typical of the Animal Style. While the horseman on one appliqué is riding towards the right, on the other he is facing left. Originally the two plates confronted one another symmetrically and were perhaps used to adorn the chest straps of a horse.

Present-day Loukovit is situated in an area which was once populated by the Triballi and the Moesians, who were Thracian tribes. Lying outside the immediate sphere of influence of the Odrysian kings, the two tribes had formed themselves by the 4th to 3rd century B.C. into an independent tribal union which even bore features of a nation-state. The military encounters with the Macedonians in the second half of the 4th century B.C. and the Celtic incursion around 280 B.C. also seriously jeopardized the regions to the north of the Balkan mountains and caused the local populace to bury their treasures. It is possible that the hoard of Loukovit was secured in this way, perhaps by a Thracian "paradynast," from alien clutches. In this context the theme of the horseman vanquishing the lion takes on an added significance, not only expressing the ritual worship of the mounted Hero but also symbolizing the power and status of the person who wore such appliqués or fastened them to his horse's bridle.

Also worthy of mention is the hoard discovered at Letnitsa, Lovech district, which—like the one at Loukovit—was a chance find. It is made up of a set of parcel-gilt silver trimmings for a horse harness which were stored in a bronze vessel. The appliqués from this find can be divided into several groups. One of these includes two ornaments in the form of a *triskele*, which was a characteristic Animal Style device, consisting of three heavily stylized griffin-head shapes (pl. **81**), and a round disk with eight fairly naturalistic horse-heads symmetrically arranged around a plain umbo (pl. **80**).

Another group is formed by five more silver plaques which share common artistic features. Four of them are very similar, showing a pair of eagles perched on either side of a fantastic plant and surmounted by two much larger griffin masks facing outwards (pl. **79**). The fifth appliqué depicts a lion locked in combat with a much larger griffin while on either side a snake joins in the struggle (pl. **85**). In both theme and design the scenes appearing on these five plaques from Letnitsa can clearly be recognized as products of the Animal Style of which, however, they reflect a further variant which appears to have been influenced even more directly than the designs considered above by Iranian or Persian-Achaemenid art.

The special significance of the Letnitsa hoard both for the history of Thracian art and for various questions concerning Thracian religion and mythology derives from a number of square and rectangular ornamental plaques with figurative reliefs. Not only, as has been mentioned several times, are scenes rarely depicted on artifacts from Thracian finds, but several illustrations on objects from the Letnitsa hoard additionally seem to form a complete cycle. Three of the plaques each portray, in a somewhat inelegant fashion, an animal combat scene: a small wolf sinks its teeth into a much larger deer (pl. **86**); two upright bears grapple with each other (pl. **88**); a stag collapses under the onslaught of a griffin (pl. **87**). Nine other plaques, which were originally affixed to the bridle straps by means of hooks, each depict a horseman in the guise of the Thracian Horseman (plates **89** to **93**). In each case the stallion is galloping along; the rider is dressed in a close-fitting suit of scale armor with long arms, leggings and foot coverings but with no helmet. With one hand he holds the reins while with the other he holds aloft a lance at the ready. Various accessories can be seen in the background: in two cases a horse's head, in two others the head of a bearded man and in one instance a woman's head. Attempts have been made to associate these scenes with accounts that the Thracians sacrificed humans and horses to their god of war in order to gain his propitiation. On the solitary plaque within this group which depicts the mounted Hero unarmed—he is holding an offering bowl in his raised right hand (pl. **94**)—the complete body of a dog can be seen above the horse's croup; thus it is more likely that it is here its master's companion and not a sacrificial offering. However, this interpretation of the relief must remain a mere hypothesis until such time as it can be checked against possible new finds.

One of the plates deviates from this pattern (pl. **95**). In places its irregular outline bears the same egg-and-dart border as the other plaques. The horseman, who is facing left, is fighting with a bear. On the ground beneath the horse's hooves lies a vanquished wolf. The rider is wearing the same type of armor as his counterparts on the other plates but in addition has a greave with a knee section in the form of a mask. It is reminiscent of the ceremonial greaves from the burials at Vratsa and Agighiol, but is less ornate. This appliqué differs from the others inasmuch as it is clearly not intended to portray the mounted Hero as an object of religious veneration but rather the real-life struggle of a man on horseback with two animals.

Some of the plaques from the Letnitsa hoard depict scenes involving several figures. One of them shows a daughter of the Greek sea-god Nereus riding on a hippocampus (pl. **97**). Religious-cum-mythological motifs also lie behind another plate (pl. **98**) which portrays a *hieros gamos*—a sacred wedding. A man and a woman are consummating their union in the presence of a second female person who is holding a palm-leaf fan over the couple. The *hieros gamos* may have been one of the elements of the myth of the Thracian Horseman. The Hero is here coupling himself with a female deity under

71 Parcel-gilt silver plaque from Letnitsa showing a human figure beside a three-headed snake (Cat. No. 2.9)

72 Bronze horse frontlet
from a grave mound near
Sofronievo (Cat. No. 1.2)

73 Silver griffin head
plaques from a grave mound
near Brezovo (Cat. No. 1.8.2)
74 Openwork silver plaques
from the grave mound at
Vratsa (Cat. No. 1.10.8)

75 Silver plaque in the form
of the forequarters of a lion
from Radyuvene (Cat. No. 2.5)
76 Silver plaque from
Loukovit (Cat. No. 2.8.3)
77 Silver horse brow-piece
from a grave mound near
Brezovo (Cat. No. 1.8.1)

78 Parcel-gilt silver
horse brow-piece from
Loukovit (Cat. No. 2.8.2)

79 Parcel-gilt silver
plaque from Letnitsa
(Cat. No. 2.9)

80 Parcel-gilt silver plaque from Letnitsa
(Cat. No. 2.9)

81 Parcel-gilt silver plaque in the form of a *triskele* from
Letnitsa (Cat. No. 2.9)

83 Parcel-gilt silver plaque from Loukovit
(Cat. No. 2.8.5)

82 Silver plaque from Loukovit (Cat. No. 2.8.4)

Preceding page

84 Parcel-gilt silver plaque from Loukovit (Cat. No. 2.8.6)

85 Parcel-gilt silver plaque from Letnitsa: a lion fighting with a griffin (Cat. No. 2.9)

86 Parcel-gilt silver plaque from Letnitsa: a wolf devouring a deer (Cat. No. 2.9)

87 Parcel-gilt silver appliqué from Letnitsa: a griffin attacking a stag (Cat. No. 2.9)

88 Parcel-gilt silver plaque from Letnitsa: two bears fighting (Cat. No. 2.9)

89—96 Parcel-gilt silver plaques depicting a horseman figure from Letnitsa (Cat. No. 2.9)

Following pages

97 Parcel-gilt silver plaque from Letnitsa: a woman astride a sea horse (Cat. No. 2.9)

98 Parcel-gilt silver plaque from Letnitsa, portraying a sacred wedding (Cat. No. 2.9)

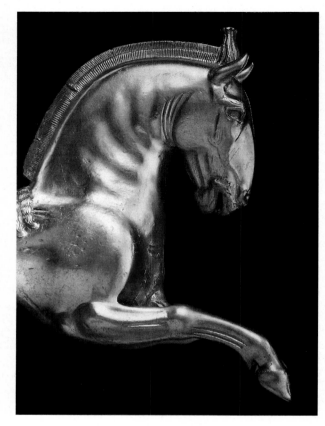

99 Partly gilt silver *rhyton* terminating in a bull *protome* (Cat. No. 2.6.3)

100 Silver *rhyton* terminating in a horse *protome*, partly gilt (Cat. No. 2.6.1)

101 Partly gilt relief on the lip of a *rhyton* terminating in a sphinx *protome* (Cat. No. 2.6.2)

102 Handle with gilt relief on a silver dish (Cat. No. 2.6.4)

103 Gilt illustration on the inside of the silver dish (Cat. No. 2.6.4)

104 Parcel-gilt silver *rhyton* in the form of a handle-less jar; portrayal of Silenus (Cat. No. 2.6.5)

105 Parcel-gilt silver *rhyton* in the form of a handle-less jar; portrayal of a dancing Cupid and a satyr playing the flute (Cat. No. 2.6.5)

106   Set of gold vessels
from Panagyurishte
(Cat. No. 2.10)

107 *Rhyton* terminating in a he-goat *protome* (Cat. No. 2.10.1)
108 *Rhyton* in the form of a ram's head (Cat. No. 2.10.4)

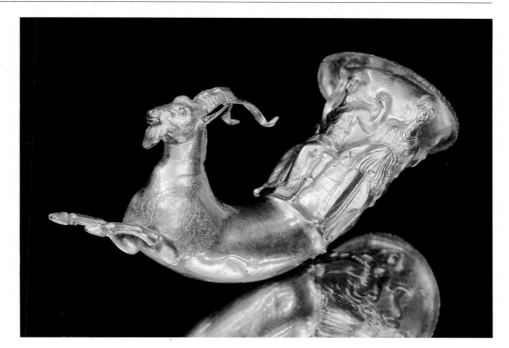

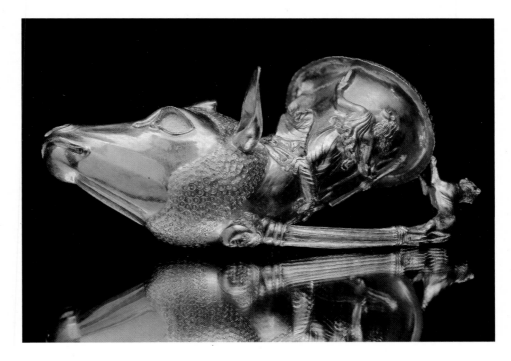

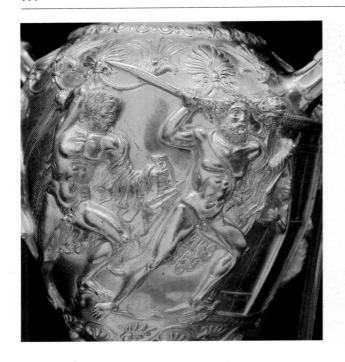

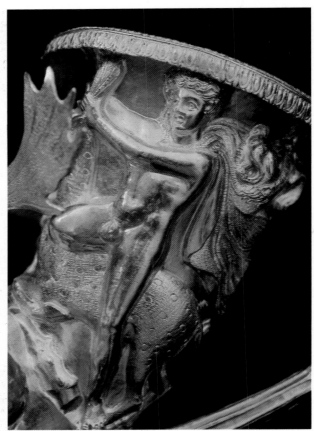

109 *Rhyton* in the form of an amphora; relief frieze on the wall (Cat. No. 2.10.8)
110 Relief below the lip of a stag's head *rhyton*: Heracles capturing the Cerynean hind (Cat. No. 2.10.3)
111 *Rhyton* resembling an amphora; handle in the form of a centaur (Cat. No. 2.10.8)

112 *Rhyton* in the form of a woman's head (Cat. No. 2.10.6)

113 Exterior of the *phiale* (Cat. No. 2.10.9)

the aegis of the Great Mother-Goddess. Through this act of consummation the Hero transcends the state of mortality and at the same time becomes the founder of a privileged race.

In view of the fact that this plaque was made at a time when not only the Odrysians but also other Thracian tribes had developed something akin to a state structure, a direct connection between the myth and the ideology of the rulers becomes evident. By claiming that he was descended from a Hero and a goddess, the king or local prince explained and legitimized his rule before the whole world.

The thematic connection between the design on this plate and other depictions of the Thracian Horseman is suggested by another plaque from the same find. It shows a horseman who has the same hairstyle as the man in the wedding scene and a gilt bow—a symbol of royal power—in the space above the horse's croup (pl. **96**). Evidently, therefore, the reliefs on the horse trappings from Letnitsa have a common thematic context, although this is not fully apparent to the modern observer. However, since there are no written records concerning Thracian mythology, as we have said before, all interpretations of the relief scenes depicted on the appliqués from Letnitsa can be no more than hypotheses. For this reason another possible interpretation will now be considered which suggests itself by a comparison with the artworks of other peoples about whose mythological beliefs more detailed information is available. According to an old Indo-European myth, Man stole the water so necessary for his survival from a triple-headed dragon which demanded, by way of expiation, regular sacrifices of young girls. It is possible that another plaque from Letnitsa depicts the arrival of such a sacrificial victim (pl. **71**).

The legend goes on to relate that a young hero set out to put an end to his people's shameful dependence on the monster, which he then fought and slew. The set of reliefs does not contain such a scene, though it is possible to see the Nereid astride the sea horse (pl. **97**) as a symbol of the freed waters. The victorious hero then weds the liberated princess (pl. **98**) and becomes the new ruler (pl. **96**).

Whatever interpretation one prefers, the close relationship between mythical and religious beliefs and the art of the Thracians—which is also reflected by the various other decorative elements for horse bridles and leather armor—is quite clear. The Animal Style with its numerous variants was a means of expression for the most diverse themes. In this respect it can thus be seen as a basic feature of Thracian art, which was closely related to the development of the power relations within Thracian society. It left its mark on the works of art manufactured during the acme of the Thracian nation-state but became less significant after Thrace was conquered by the Macedonians.

The Silver Drinking Vessels from Borovo

8

In the course of ploughing a field near the village of Borovo, Rousse district, in 1974 two silver *rhyta* as well as fragments of a bowl on a dish *(podanypter)* came to light. The area was at once thoroughly excavated, and this led to the discovery of another *rhyton* and a jar decorated with reliefs. In the vicinity of the find there are several grave mounds, and at first it was assumed that the silverware had originally been interred as grave goods. Detailed investigations, however, showed that the objects had been buried in the ground as a hoard. The rims of some of the vessels bore inscriptions whose content and technique resembled closely a number of *phialai* from the richly adorned mounds at Vratsa and Agighiol. Like these latter finds, the silver vessels from Borovo have been dated to the first half of the 4th century B.C. and are thus a further testimony to the economic, political and cultural highpoint which the Thracian state had then attained.

The three drinking horns form part of a group of *rhyta* with relatively small *protomai* and elongated, fluted bodies. One *rhyton* has the form of a winged sphinx while the other two are depicted as animal *protomai*, one as a horse and the other as a bull. The drinking horn which terminates in an equine *protome* (pl. **100**)—its mane and neck-folds as well as the pouring hole in the form of a lion's head situated between the animal's outstretched forelegs are all gilt—bears vertical fluting, as does the sphinx *rhyton*. Around the upper rim of both vessels runs a gilt bas-relief showing an ivy creeper on which, in the case of the sphinx *rhyton*, a little bird is perched (pl. **101**).

The style of the bovine *rhyton* clearly reveals an Oriental influence (pl. **99**) which is particularly apparent in the squat form of the animal's body, its folded legs (between which the pouring hole is again situated) and the strongly stylized portrayal of the gilt hair on the bull's hide. The horizontal fluting is also a departure from the normal pattern and serves to accentuate the squatness of the main vessel, the rim of which is ornamented only by a simple palmette.

The large silver bowl was originally used for serving the mixed wine. This is indicated by the bearded silenus head with the typically pointed ears on the wall of the vessel just below the handles (pl. **102**). The interior of the vessel shows an animal scene (pl. **103**) fashioned in the same artistic manner as the trimmings for weaponry and horse harnesses. A deer succumbs to the assault of a griffin which has sunk its claws into its victim's shoulders and is pecking at its head with its beak. The chasework gilt relief appears on the base of the bowl.

The main item in the Borovo treasure is a handle-less *rhyton* just 18 cm high. The drinking hole is situated at the sharply tapering base of the vessel and is framed by three flying swans. A double frieze richly adorned with figures appears to hover on the swans' wings. The theme is taken from the myths surrounding Dionysus, the god of wine. In the center of the lower group of figures sits a bearded Dionysus in full face (pl. **114**). He wears a wreath of ivy in his hair, has a small *phiale* in his left hand and in his right a *rhyton*, which resembles the sphinx *rhyton* described above. To his right is seated a woman dressed after the Greek fashion in a chiton; she proffers a decorated ribbon to a winged Cupid who stands before her. She is Ariadne, the princess born on the island of Crete who helped the Attic hero Theseus to slay the Minotaur and to find his way out of the laby-

114 Parcel-gilt silver *rhyton* in the form of a handle-less jar; representation of Dionysus and Ariadne (Cat. No. 2.6.5)

rinth. Later he treacherously deserted her on the island of Naxos where Dionysus found her and made her his wife. Their wedding forms the subject of the scene represented on the *rhyton*.

Behind Dionysus sits Silenus, the god's former tutor and later companion, in a very relaxed posture on a rock covered with the hide of a panther (pl. **104**). He too is wearing ivy leaves in his hair. In his left hand he has a small *phiale* while with the other he holds aloft a *rhyton* which terminates in the *protome* of a winged lion. The whole demeanor of Silenus suggests that he is in his habitual state of drunkenness.

The lower frieze also shows a satyr playing a double-reeded flute while a winged Cupid performs a ritual dance (pl. **105**). The upper, smaller frieze depicts various companions of Dionysus, satyrs and maenads, who form a troupe of dancers and musicians enveloping a patient and tranquil couple. The man and woman are being initiated via certain rituals into the mysteries of the Dionysian cult and accepted into the ranks of the wine-god's followers.

On the neck of the *rhyton* is engraved a Greek inscription which contains two names; one of them, Kotys, may well refer to the Odrysian king Kotys I (383 to 359 B.C.). This enables us to date the whole find to the first half of the 4th century B.C. The same inscription reoccurs on the *rhyton* with an equine *protome* from Borovo and on some *phialai* from the richly furnished graves of Vratsa and Agighiol. Perhaps the Odrysian king gave these valuable objects as presents to the chieftains of some of the other Thracian tribes in order to secure their loyalty.

Each of the drinking vessels and the reliefs depicted on them portrays Dionysus, the son of the god Zeus and the mortal Semele. In Homer's day he was not yet counted as one of the Olympian gods. Not until the 6th century B.C. was he accepted into the official Greek cult, but he soon enjoyed great popularity since, unlike most other Olympians, he constantly mixed among mortal men and let them partake of his gifts—the vine and its intoxicating product. His triumphant advance began in Thrace, where he is said to have grown up and to have planted the first vines; later his influence spread as far as India.

Like other deities Dionysus possessed various, in part contradictory, characteristics. The Thracians saw him as the bringer of the vine and thus as a god of fertility and vegetation in whose honor people—especially women—went into ecstatic trances. When in such a frenzy they were capable of tearing apart animals or even people who tried to interfere with their pleasure. But the Thracians also ascribed another power to him: high up in the Thracian mountains sacred shrines were set up to which people came from near and far to consult the god about their future. The most famous visitors in the history of the Dionysiac oracle in Thrace, the location of which has still not been determined, were undoubtedly Alexander the Great (336 to 323 B.C.) and the father of the Roman emperor Augustus (27 B.C. to A.D. 14), who were informed of the god's prophecies by the officiating priest.

However, the set of silver drinking vessels from Borovo were indubitably used in rituals dedicated to Dionysus in his function of the merry wine-god. In this guise he can also be seen as the personification of the Thracians' fondness for alcoholic indulgence, for which they were renowned—not to say notorious—among their contemporaries. The figure of Dionysus also reflects the long-established relations between the Thracians and their Greek neighbors in the cultural sphere.

9

The Gold Hoard of Panagyurishte

While excavating loam at a brickworks near Panagyurishte, Plovdiv district, on 8 December 1949 a group of workers came across some gold vessels and thus discovered one of the most significant treasure troves from Thrace ever found. Subsequent archaeological investigations failed to uncover any further information concerning the site, so that this hoard must also be classified as a one-off chance find.

The treasure includes a *phiale*, three animal head *rhyta*, a drinking horn terminating in an animal *protome*, three *rhyta* in the form of female heads and an amphora with two pouring holes (pl. **106**). With a total weight of 6.1 kg these vessels of pure gold foil constitute an extraordinarily rich treasure. In addition, the ornamental and figurative designs embossed on each vessel have a priceless cultural value. The style of the reliefs relates closely to Greek art from the late 4th to the early 3rd century B.C., and so the Panagyurishte hoard can also be dated to this period. The themes depicted likewise evince a Greek influence and are largely drawn from the world of Greek myths and sagas.

On the upper part of a *rhyton* with a stag's head finial (pl. **106**, left foreground) is a four-figure scene which depicts the Judgement of Paris. Paris, the son of the Trojan king, had to decide who was the most beautiful of the three goddesses Hera, Athena and Aphrodite. He opted for Aphrodite who as a reward—not to say bribe—promised him Helen, the most beautiful woman on earth. But Helen was the wife of Menelaus, the brother of the king of Mycenae, and Paris had to abduct her from the Greek mainland. Menelaus, with the support of his brother Agamemnon and other Achaean princes, then set out on a campaign of vengeance against Troy which ended ten years later with the destruction of the city. This pictorial illustration of the mythical background of the Trojan War also bore significance for the Thracians, since some of them had themselves taken part in the military conflicts between the Mycenaean empire and Troy.

The second drinking horn in the form of a stag's head with heavy antlers portrays two Greek heroes: Theseus, who is shown killing the bull of Marathon, and Heracles, who was very popular among the Thracians, whom we see catching the Cerynean hind with its golden horns (pl. **110**). This was one of the twelve labors which Heracles had to perform on behalf of Eurystheus and which constitute the core of the Greek Heraclean myth.

The third vessel in this group has the form of a ram's head (pl. **108**) whose woolly hide is indicated by a series of ovules. The pouring hole is situated between the animal's flews in each case. All three *rhyta* have a handle which is fixed to the wall of the vessel in the form of a mask while terminating at the other end in the figure of a lion with its front claws resting on the lip. The relief which appears on the ram's head *rhyton* also derives from Greek mythology and shows Dionysus in the company of the maenad Eriope flanked by two more maenads dancing ecstatically.

Another *rhyton* has the *protome* of a horned billy-goat with a bung-hole between its front legs. Its body merges into the curved, handle-less wall of the drinking horn on which a four-figure relief is depicted (pl. **107**). The scene is dominated by the figure of Hera who with her left hand is lifting her veil while in the right she holds an offering bowl—a pose commonly used in Greek art to depict women or goddesses making a ritual offering. On one side of her throne stands the goddess Artemis and on the other the latter's brother Apollo. The two each carry a bow. On the reverse of the vessel opposite the figure of Hera appears Nike, the goddess of victory. Greek inscriptions name all four figures.

No myth exists which directly relates these four gods to one another. Artemis, Apollo and Hera were worshipped not only by the Greeks but also by the Thracians, and portrayals of Nike also occur in Thracian art. The juxtaposition of these four deities, who are not linked together by any common activity, suggests that a non-Greek, possibly a Thracian, toreut simply included various mythological figures known to him within a single frieze. Several shortcomings in the representation of the figures, e.g. the awkwardly portrayed left arm of Hera or the organically inaccurate posture of Heracles' right leg on the stag's head *rhyton*, likewise suggest that it was the work of a goldsmith who, though having made a careful study of Greek art, lacked the anatomical knowledge that a native Greek craftsman would have had.

Another group of drinking vessels comprises three *rhyta* with flat bases. In each case the wall of the vessel has the form of a woman's head out of whose hair grows the smooth, cylindrical neck (pl. **112**), rather like the caryatids which occur in Greek architecture. Emerging from the back of the head is a four-sided, fluted handle, the upper part of which is designed as a winged sphinx with its claws resting on the lip of the vessel. The neck of each woman is adorned with a band bearing a lion's head medallion which conceals the pouring hole.

Two of the figures wear hairnets with a star pattern; the hair of the third is largely concealed by a helmet decorated with two griffins (pl. **106**, to the right of the *phiale*). At first these three figures were seen as representatives of the Amazons, the mythological men-hating tribe of women, but today it is thought that they depict the three goddesses Hera, Aphrodite and Athena. This assumption is based primarily on the widespread typification of Athena as a helmeted figure, whereas the other two female heads have no unmistakable attributes which would identify them as Hera and Aphrodite.

Rhyta in the form of amphorae are unusual inasmuch as they represent the fusion of two types of vessel with different functions—a drinking cup and a storage vessel. However, this form reoccurs among Thracian finds: the Achaemenid amphora from the cemetery at Douvanli (pl. **21**) and the *rhyton* from Borovo made in a Thracian workshop (plates **104**, **105**, **114**) have already been dealt with. The third such example is the amphora/*rhyton* from Panagyurishte (pl. **106**, left background). It has a smooth neck with an everted lip which, like the rims of the *rhyta* designed as animal and women's heads, is decorated with an egg-and-dart and beaded ornament. This same pattern on the rim clearly shows that all these vessels originally belonged together. The fluted handles of the amphora terminate in two centaurs (pl. **111**), which face each other with arms raised in pugnacious fashion. The centaur—a mythological creature consisting of the torso of a man and the body of a horse—was a frequently depicted subject in Greek art. It was a popular motif among Thracian craftsmen both because they enjoyed portraying mythological themes and because of the high esteem in which the horse was held.

The amphora from the Panagyurishte hoard, like the silver *rhyton* from Borovo, bears an elaborate scene depicted in relief (pl. **109**). The centerpiece of this animated scene is formed by a set of double doors studded with decorative nails and framed by Ionic columns and an ornamental border (far right in picture). One door is ajar and a bearded old man is peering out anxiously, for from the left four men armed with swords are advancing menacingly. Each man is naked apart from a cloak which flows behind him, and they are all marching forward in unison. They differ only in the posture of their sword-bearing arm. The uneven contours beneath their feet indicate that the attackers are on hilly ground outside the palace. They are being egged on from behind by a fifth, motionless man who is blowing on a battle horn. He stands back to back with another, older man who is engrossed in a conversation with a younger companion.

Their relaxed conversation is taking place behind the palace, as it were, for they are separated from the combatants by the large portal. Their non-participation in the attack is further underlined by the fact that they are carrying a knotty stick and a sheathed sword.

As yet no explanation has been forthcoming for the frieze depicted on the amphora/*rhyton*. Perhaps it is a somewhat idiosyncratic representation of the Greek saga of the attack by the Seven against Thebes, or possibly it was meant as an illustration of some Thracian myth of which we are ignorant.

Above the figures is a frieze of palmettes and lotus blossoms and below is a border of trailing palmettes. Around the base of the amphora are more reliefs which are again taken from the myths of Dionysus and Heracles. Silenus, the tutor of Dionysus, stands holding a double-reeded flute and a *kantharos* opposite a youthful Heracles, who is strangling two snakes with his child's hands. They were sent by the jealous Hera in order to kill the child, the offspring of the union between her lawful husband Zeus and the mortal Alcmene. Interspersed in this frieze, beneath each handle, is the head of a negro which conceals a pouring hole.

It was rare for a *rhyton* to have two bung-holes, so it is possible that the vessel in question had to serve a special function. Among the Thracians the conclusion of every treaty or the affirmation of a fraternal alliance for common political or military purposes was always accompanied by ritual ceremonies, as was also customary among their various neighbors. The Thracians therefore thought it only right and proper for both parties to the contract to drink simultaneously from the same vessel in order to demonstrate their unity before the gods and their fellow men. It must have been on such occasions, which reflect the interrelationship between politics and cult rituals, that the amphora/*rhyton* was used. Having defined the function of this one vessel, it is safe to assume that the other vessels served the same purpose, since their common form and style clearly indicate that they belonged to one and the same set.

The ninth vessel of the Panagyurishte hoard, the *phiale* (pl. **113**), served a purpose closely related to that of the eight drinking vessels. The bowl was used for making ritual offerings to the gods so that they would graciously vouchsafe the projects of their mortal subjects. Its outer surface is adorned by several friezes around the smooth *omphalos*. The innermost circle consists of

rosettes and the second of acorns—two motifs which constantly reoccur in Thracian art. Outside these are three circles of negro heads. Their broad, flat noses, fleshy lips and short, curly hair give them a realistic appearance, while stylistically they resemble the two negro heads that conceal the bung-holes on the amphora/*rhyton*.

The treasure of Panagyurishte thus represents an integrated set of vessels which were once employed for certain ritual ceremonies. The motifs and style clearly indicate Greek influence, though some shortcomings in the execution strongly suggest that the items were made in a non-Greek workshop. The form of some of the vessels derives partly from Oriental art.

In seeking to locate the site of manufacture of these vessels, we can draw on some marks etched into the amphora/*rhyton* and the *phiale* which have been identified as Greek weight specifications. The Greeks used gold coins (*stater*) as the units of weight for gold objects, yet this weight varied from one mint to another. A comparison of the actual weight of the vessels with the units of weights and measures employed in antiquity suggests that it was most probably the *stater* minted in Lampsacus which served as the basic unit of weight in the case of the *phiale* and the amphora/*rhyton* from Panagyurishte. Lampsacus was a Greek colony on the Asiatic side of the Dardanelles founded by the Ionian town of Phokaia. The geographical position of the town as well as its history created a favorable basis for the development of a local style of craftsmanship which fused the traditions of Greece and Asia Minor into a new style which also suited the tastes of the Thracian clients.

The Panagyurishte hoard has been dated to the late 4th or early 3rd century B.C., i.e. in the latter years of the golden age of Thracian culture. It was a period characterized by military conflicts with Alexander the Great, which led to Thrace being incorporated into the Macedonian empire; by armed struggle following the death of Alexander in 323 B.C. against Lysimachus, a former general under Alexander who later became king of Thrace, which lasted until his death in 281 B.C.; and by the Celtic invasion of the Balkan peninsula which followed almost immediately. Against this background of constant turbulence it is understandable that the owner or custodian of this treasure, which is immensely valuable both in material terms and in its artistic and cultural significance, should have sought to prevent its loss or destruction by burying the hoard in a place from which it was not recovered until more than 2,000 years later.

Catalog

The following catalog lists all the items mentioned in the preceding text and shown in the illustrations. However, this time they are not divided into categories; instead all the objects from a particular find are listed together. The inventories of burial sites are given first, followed by the chance discoveries of treasure and then the one-off individual finds. Within these groups the finds are arranged chronologically as far as possible. In documenting the burial sites all the objects found in the same grave are enumerated in order to give the reader an overall impression of the way Thracian tombs were furnished.

The following abbreviations have been used:

W	Width
Dm	Diameter
H	Height
Inv. No.	Inventory number under which the item is listed in the respective museum catalog
L	Length
Ldm	Diameter of the lip

1. Burial finds

1.1   From the great complex of finds unearthed at the Eneolithic necropolis near Varna, which has been dated to between 3200 and 3000 B.C., only a few grave goods can be mentioned here. In addition the graves contained various bangles, necklaces, rings, diadems, copper axes, copper needles, flint blades, a gold replica of a vertebra which was used as a wedge and a small marble bowl. All these objects are today in the Archaeological Museum, Varna.

1.1.1   Gold appliqués in various forms
24 round convex disks
Dm 1.3–2.2 cm; Inv. No. I-1531
6 trapezoid plaques
H 1.2–1.5 cm; Inv. No. I-1529
4 crescent-shaped plaques
L 3.5–3.7 cm; Inv. No. I-1527
7 round convex amulets with hooks
Dm 1.5–2.0 cm; Inv. No. I-1652
30 disks in the form of stylized horned animal heads
L 2.8–4.0 cm, H 1.2–2.1 cm; Inv. No. I-1657
Plate **27**

1.1.2   The figure of a bull of stamped gold foil
L 6.5 cm, H 5.8 cm; Inv. No. I-1633
Plate **5**

1.1.3   Face mask of unbaked clay, from one of the symbolic graves. Eyes, lips and teeth marked by gold strips; on the forehead was a diadem; earrings; around the neck were several gold amulets.
Plate **28**

1.1.4   Fragments of a gold foil covering for a scepter
L 22.5 cm, W 5.3 cm; Inv. No. I-1641–1649
Plate **6**

1.2   A small grave mound was examined near the village of Sofronievo, Vratsa district, dating from the 6th century B.C. Beneath a layer of flints lay the cremated remains of a man and a horse. The burial accessories consisted of: 1 set of bronze horse bridle trappings, 1 bronze snaffle, 1 bronze *phiale*, 1 bronze fibula, 1 bronze arm bangle, 1 bronze belt clasp, 1 bronze button, 1 iron knife, 2 iron spearheads, 1 iron chain. All these objects are today in the Historical Museum, Vratsa.

Bronze horse frontlet
L 8.5 cm, W 6.5 cm, H 3.5 cm; Inv. No. 757
Plate **72**

1.3 The necropolis near Douvanli

In the vicinity of the village of Douvanli, Plovdiv district, lies a necropolis containing some 50 grave mounds. In 1925 a stone grave was discovered by chance at the periphery of the largest mound—the Koukova Mogila. Systematic excavations began in 1929, and today the majority of the mounds have been investigated.

The 15 meter-high Koukova Mogila occupied a special position within the necropolis as a whole. Among the bottom-most layers of the mound were remains of a Bronze Age settlement, including a tomb dating from that period. The whole barrow was honeycombed with various large offering pits in which charred remains, bones and potsherds from the 1st millennium B.C. were found. This barrow probably had a central function in connection with the burial cult for the whole necropolis, for it was not originally raised as a grave mound. The stone grave, which was found by chance, was only inserted after the construction of the barrow. A woman was buried there at the start of the 5th century B.C. along with a rich array of burial gifts: 1 gold torque, 1 necklace of gold pearls, 1 gold pendant, 2 gold bracelets, 11 gold earrings, 2 gold finger-rings, 1 gold pectoral, 3 fish of stamped gold foil, 2 silver vessels, 5 bronze vessels, 1 bronze mirror, 1 iron tripod, 1 alabaster jar, 5 Greek clay vessels.

1.3.1 Parcel-gilt silver amphora
H 27 cm, Ldm 13.4 cm
Archaeological Museum, Sofia; Inv. No. 6137
Plates **21/22**

Beneath another grave mound—the Mushovitsa Mogila—lay the oldest burial in the necropolis of Douvanli which dates from the end of the 6th century B.C., a time when Thrace was ruled by the Persian king. The barrow has a diameter of 32 m and at the start of the excavations was about 4 m high. The tomb was situated right at the center of the barrow at ground level: a wooden coffin lay in a simple earth pit which contained a female skeleton. Apart from one clay vessel, all the grave goods were arranged around the woman's head: 2 necklaces of variously shaped gold pearls, 10 gold earrings and 2 hook-like pendants, 1 gold pectoral, 1 silver *phiale* that acted as the lid of a bronze *hydria*, 1 bronze mirror, 1 female clay figurine, 3 Grecian clay vessels, some local pottery, a number of clay amulets, 3 glass jars, 7 alabaster jars with hooks for hanging them up with and several decorative plaques, stone ornaments, isolated pearls etc. Overall the grave furnishings are similar to those of the tomb in the Koukova Mogila.

1.3.2 10 similar gold earrings
L 2.7–3.2 cm
Archaeological Museum, Plovdiv; Inv. No. 1537
Plate **37**

1.3.3 Gold pectoral
L 25.9 cm
Archaeological Museum, Plovdiv; Inv. No. 1531
Plate **44**

The Bashova Mogila had a diameter of 35 m and a height of 6 m, though in the course of the excavations in October 1929 it was completely levelled. Within the mound a sacrificial pit was found which was similar to the one in the Koukova Mogila. The burial chamber was made of ashlars of which only the inner surfaces were smooth. It was covered by several heavy wooden beams. In the tomb the remains of a cremation were found in a silver bowl. The following burial gifts were interred along with the deceased: 1 gold pectoral, 4 parcel-gilt silver vessels on each of which was engraved in Greek letters the name of the owner, i.e. of the deceased: Dadamele; there were also 5 bronze vessels, 1 suit of bronze armor with an iron belt, 40 bronze arrowheads, 2 iron spearheads, 1 iron sword, 1 iron dagger sheath (the dagger itself has disintegrated) and 3 Grecian clay vessels.

1.3.4 Parcel-gilt silver *rhyton* terminating in a horse *protome*
H 20.6 cm
Archaeological Museum, Plovdiv; Inv. No. 1517
Inside the lip is the inscription DADAMELE.
Plate **24**

1.3.5 Gold pectoral
L 13.8 cm, H 13.8 cm
Archaeological Museum, Plovdiv; Inv. No. 1514
Plate **41**

1.4 Construction workers in Staro Selo, Sliven district,

stumbled across a tomb that dated back to the first half of the 5th century B.C. In the course of the centuries the mound of earth with which it had been covered had been levelled out, but the grave goods were recovered and are today in the Archaeological Museum, Sofia: 1 gold pectoral, 1 cylindrical silver goblet, 3 bronze vessels, 1 bronze tripod, 6 black varnished drinking cups imported from Greece.

Gold pectoral decorated with a relief
L 17 cm, H 11 cm;
Inv. No. 8123
Plate **42**

1.5 In a barrow at Boukyovtsi, Varna district, dating from the turn of the 5th/4th centuries B.C. the following items were found: several silver fittings for a horse harness, 2 silver *phialai*, 1 silver cup, 1 silver jar and 2 silver handles (the vessels of which they were part have been lost). All these items are now kept in the Archaeological Museum, Sofia.

1.5.1 Silver *phiale*
Dm 13 cm, H 5.5 cm; Inv. No. 6697
Plate **16**

In the same area another grave mound from the 4th century B.C. was examined. Several silver vessels and a decorative silver breastplate with an unusual form came to light.

1.5.2 Silver breastplate consisting of 6 fibulae, several chains with acorn and poppy capsule pendants and interconnecting links in the form of human masks and rosettes
Archaeological Museum, Sofia; Inv. No. 2558-A
Plate **65**

1.6 A grave mound from the 4th century B.C. was investigated near Agighiol, Tulcea district (Romania). Beneath the mound lay a walled tomb consisting of a long passage *(dromos)* and two burial chambers. In the burial chambers were the skeletons of a man and three horses. The following grave goods were recovered: 1 silver, parcel-gilt ceremonial helmet, 2 silver greaves with traces of gilding, various gold earrings, 2 silver goblets, 4 silver *phialai*, 1 *phiale* of cast bronze, 2 gold foil appliqués, several silver horse bridle trappings, bronze and iron arrowheads and spearheads, a number of slingshot stones and Greek clay vessels from the late 5th century B.C. All these objects are today in the Danube-Delta Museum, Tulcea; Inv. Nos. 11850–11857, 11859–11872.

1.6.1 Silver, parcel-gilt ceremonial helmet with embossed relief
H 27 cm
Plate **68**

1.6.2 Two parcel-gilt silver greaves with embossed reliefs
H 47.8 and 46 cm
Plate **69**

1.7 Near Ruets, Turgovishte district, a burial chamber consisting of ashlars was found in a barrow measuring 45 m in diameter and 8 m in height. There were no traces of the burial itself, but judging by the grave goods it must have been a male burial dating from around 400 B.C. All the items are today in the Archaeological Museum, Sofia: 1 bronze cuirass, 1 bronze helmet, 1 iron sword, 11 bronze arrowheads, 1 iron spear-

head, 3 bronze vessels, 2 decorated bone handles, 1 glass vessel and 1 fragment of a Greek vase with red figures depicted on it.

Bronze cuirass
H 35 cm; Inv. No. 6168
Plate **51**

1.8 Inside a grave mound near Brezovo, Plovdiv district, which was raised at the turn of the 5th/4th centuries B.C. 2 silver *phialai*, 1 gold finger-ring and 1 set of decorative horse bridle trappings were found. The objects are today in the Archaeological Museum, Sofia.

1.8.1 Silver brow-piece for a horse
H 4.7 cm; Inv. No. 1712
Plate **77**

1.8.2 4 silver plaques in the form of griffin heads which were arranged in two pairs
H 4.5–4.8 cm; Inv. No. 1712
Plate **73**

1.9 Near the village of Rozovets, Plovdiv district, lie three tumuli of which the largest measures 30 m in diameter and 8 m in height. In 1851 a round burial chamber constructed of marble blocks was discovered there. The chamber probably had a vaulted ceiling originally. Reputedly the burial chamber contained a skeleton with a bronze helmet on its head and a suit of iron armor on its chest. However, details of the discovery and of the burial treasure are very sketchy. It is probable that the grave contained the following items: 1 gold signet ring, 3 silver *phialai*, 5 bronze vessels, 1 gold laurel wreath, 2 Greek clay vessels, 2 locally produced clay vessels and some 500 bronze arrowheads.

As a result of this discovery the Turkish government, which at the time ruled Bulgaria, ordered the neighboring barrows to be thoroughly investigated; after the liberation of Bulgaria in 1878 the work was continued under Russian supervision. The tomb found beneath the southern barrow within this group was furnished similarly to the first grave: 4 silver vessels, 10 silver appliqués, 1 iron sword, 1 iron spearhead, the remains of a bronze helmet and 2 clay vessels imported from Greece which enable us to date the grave to the early 4th century B.C.

Parcel-gilt silver *rhyton* in the form of a deer's head
H 11.2 cm, Ldm 9 cm
Archaeological Museum, Sofia; Inv. No. B-49
Plate **23**

1.10 In 1965, in preparation for construction work in Vratsa, one of the most significant of the Thracian grave mounds—the Mogilanska Mogila—was examined. Beneath the earth-mound lay three tombs of which the oldest dates from the second quarter of the 4th century B.C. and the youngest some 30 years later. One round burial chamber made of fluvial rocks had already been completely ransacked in antiquity. A second, rectangular chamber had also been robbed—the tunnel which the thieves had used to gain access to the grave was clearly discernible—but they left some of the grave goods behind. In this room two people had been buried, a man and a woman, which is evident from the remaining grave goods: 1 bronze fibula, 1 bronze ring, parts of a gold necklace, bronze fittings for a wooden box. Local and Greek pottery lay along one side of the burial chamber while near the opposite wall were found 1 quiver with 73 bronze arrowheads, 2 iron knives and various clay amulets. Separate from these two groups of objects one silver and one gold jar were also found.

1.10.1 Gold jar decorated with a relief
H 9 cm
Historical Museum, Vratsa; Inv. No. B-391
Plate **19**

1.10.2 Gilt silver jar
H 8 cm
Historical Museum, Vratsa; Inv. No. B-392
Plate **25**, left

The third burial under the Mogilanska Mogila lay in a rectangular burial chamber and had been undisturbed by robbers. Here lay the skeletons of two horses which had been harnessed up to a four-wheeled chariot. Their bridles were unadorned, in contrast to that of a third horse which lay apart from the other two and had been a charger. Its harness had been decorated with 11 silver plaques. Near the horses lay the skeleton of a man, and next to him were found 1 bronze fibula, 18 arrowheads and a number of slingshot stones.

In the same room but apart from the others lay the skeleton of a woman in the vicinity of which the majority of the grave goods were found, including parts of armor and weapons: 1 gold laurel wreath, gold earrings, 1 bronze earring, glass and bronze pearls from a necklace, 1 bronze fibula, several clay amulets; there were also 2 iron knives, approximately 100 arrowheads, 1 gilt greave of embossed silver foil, 1 bronze helmet. At a little distance away from the woman two silver jars, 4 silver *phialai*, 1 bronze jar, 2 bronze *situlae* and 1 iron candelabra were also found.

1.10.3 Silver *phiale* with a gilt medallion on its umbo depicting the goddess Aphrodite
Dm 10 cm, H 4.5 cm
Historical Museum, Vratsa; Inv. No. B-68
Plate **15**

1.10.4 Silver jar which in shape and decoration resembles a pine-cone
H 14 cm, Ldm 6 cm
Historical Museum, Vratsa; Inv. No. B-66
Plate **25**, background

1.10.5 Laurel wreath of gold foil
Dm 24 cm
Historical Museum, Vratsa; Inv. No. B-59
Plate **33**

1.10.6 Two gold earrings with pendants
L 7.5 cm
Historical Museum, Vratsa; Inv. No. B-60
Plate **36**

1.10.7 Parcel-gilt silver greaves
H 46 cm
Historical Museum, Vratsa; Inv. No. B-231
Plates **56/57**

1.10.8 2 silver plaques
H 8.5 cm
Historical Museum, Vratsa; Inv. No. B-38,39
Plate **74**

1.10.9 Silver jar
H 16.5 cm, Ldm 9 cm
Historical Museum, Vratsa; Inv. No. B-67
Plate **25**, right

1.11 Among several tumuli in the vicinity of the village of Metsek, Haskovo district, the most significant is the so-called Mal-Tepe (treasure mound). It is 90 m in diameter and 14 m high. The earth-mound was held in place by a broad band of rocks. Between 1931 and 1933 the largest vaulted tomb in Bulgaria was uncovered beneath this mound. It consists of a passage (*dromos*) 21.5 m long and 2.6 m high, 2 rectangular side chambers more than 3 m high (1.5×1.2 and 1.8×2.1 m respectively) and a round main burial chamber with a diameter of 3.3 m with a beehive dome. The entire tomb was constructed of ashlars. The round chamber was sealed by a decorated bronze door. Opposite the entrance stood a stone deathbed next to which were two stone chests. Yet no skeleton was found, and the grave goods lay scattered around the whole room. For reasons unknown the burial was removed or destroyed way back in antiquity. The following objects were recovered: 11 gold appliqués, 1 gold decorative plate with cornelian inlays, gold pearls from two necklaces, 3 gold fingerrings, 1 bronze statue of a boar, 1 silver plaque, 1 silver *phiale*, 2 bronze candelabras, 3 bronze lamps, 8 bronze vessels, several bronze fittings from the entrance door and from a chariot, 1 iron ceremonial breastplate overlaid with gilt silver foil, 2 iron swords, 1 iron spearhead, 3 glass pearls, 3 clay vessels, 1 clay amulet. These objects suggest a male burial. In the rectangular anterooms two cremated female burials were found which were likewise richly furnished with grave goods. In one of the graves were found: 1 gold decorative plaque with cornelian inlays which was very similar to the one found in the rotunda, 23 gold pearls, 2 glass chain pendants, 6 gilt clay pearls, 1 clay whorl, 1 bronze button and 1 Greek silver coin minted in the reign of Alexander the Great (336 to 323 B.C.). In the other grave there was another silver drachma depicting Alexander the Great; 14 gold chain links with filigree work plus 1 gold pendant, gold pearls from another necklace, 1 gold chain, 7 gold earrings, 3 gold plaques, 1 gold button, 1 silver needle, 1 glass jar, 2 glass pearls, 35 parcel-gilt clay pearls, 1 clay whorl and 1 iron knife.

The coins allow us to date both cremations to the last quarter of the 4th century B.C., while the grave in the main chamber is somewhat older. All the items listed are now in the Archaeological Museum, Sofia.

1.11.1 Gold ornaments from various tombs beneath the Mal-Tepe of Metsek arranged in a decorative set
2 appliqués with plant motifs from the round main chamber
H 3.4 cm; Inv. No. 6452
4 round ornamental disks with rosette ornaments from the round chamber
Dm 2.2–2.8 cm; Inv. No. 6453
Necklace with pendant. The pearls and pendant were found in one of the cremations, the terminals in the other cremation.
Inv. Nos. 6426, 6428
5 earrings with lion masks, from one of the cremations
Dm 2.0–2.2 cm; Inv. No. 6442
Plate **29**

1.11.2 Iron pectoral coated with gilt silver foil, from the male burial
L 29 cm; Inv. No. 6401
Plate **43**

1.11.3 5 decorated halter rings from a four-wheeled chariot, from the round burial chamber
H 7.3–8.4 cm; Inv. Nos. 6411, 6412
Plate **47**

1.12 In a grave mound near Panagyurishte, Plovdiv district, the following objects, which are today housed in the Archaeological Museum in Sofia, were discovered: 2 gold belt fittings, 2 gold plaques, 2 gold buttons with an Apollo mask in relief, 4 gold nails for the securing of various appliqués, 6 square silver plaques which also bore Apollo reliefs, 7 round silver disks showing Heracles slaying the Nemean lion or decorated with animal or plant designs, 1 elongated silver fitting with figurative reliefs, 1 silver jar, 2 silver *phialai*, 2 bronze plaques, 6 bronze vessels, links from a bronze chain, 10 iron arrowheads and spearheads, 2 iron horse snaffles and 2 unpainted clay amphorae. The tomb has been dated to the 4th or 3rd century B.C.

1.12.1 Silver shield plaque
L 32 cm, W 6.7–12 cm; Inv. No. 3555
Plate **58**

1.12.2 2 similar round silver disks
Dm 8 cm; Inv. No. 3561
Plate **59**

1.12.3 2 horse bridle trappings, copper and silver alloy
H 6.1 cm; Inv. No. 3569
Plate **70**

1.13 Near the Thracian royal residential town of Seuthopolis, in what is today Kazanluk, a vaulted tomb was found which had been robbed back in antiquity. It consists of a square antechamber, a *dromos* and a round burial chamber with two deathbeds. The antechamber (2.6 × 1.4 m) has a flat ceiling, the *dromos* (1.9 × 1.1 m, H 2.25 m) a tent-shaped ceiling and the round burial chamber (Dm 2.65 m) has a beehive roof (H 3.25 m). This dome is built according to the so-called false vault principle, i.e. of bricks each layer of which juts out above the underlying one. The walls of the *dromos* and the burial chamber are painted in the style of Greek murals of the early 3rd century B.C. In the *dromos* is a Pompeiian red border above which runs a band of plant ornaments surmounted by a frieze depicting battle scenes. The lower part of the wall of the burial chamber is also red. Inside the cupola are two friezes depicting figures bordered by several ornamental bands. The main frieze shows a man and a woman—possibly the couple who were buried here—at a wake flanked by male and female servants bringing various gifts. The smaller frieze portrays a chariot race with three wagons each being pulled by four horses—probably an illustration of the funerary games held as part of the funeral ceremony.
Plate **3**

1.14   At the beginning of this century a flurry of construction work was carried out on the small peninsula of Nessebur in Bourgas district. During excavation work a large number of graves made of simple large stone slabs were discovered. Originally wooden coffins lay in these stone tombs. The necropolis of the former Thracian town of Messambria had been found. In the following decades it was investigated insofar as the new buildings above the surface allowed this. Many of these tombs contained lavish grave goods which apparently were placed alongside the deceased according to a standard ritual. Thus the female burials nearly all contained a clay jar which had been broken before being put into the tomb. Another feature of the female burials were bronze mirrors and clay vessels decorated with reliefs—so-called Megarian goblets—while most of the male graves contained an iron scraper.

The uniformity of the jars in the female burials indicates that they were all relatively contemporaneous and, on the other hand, that they were manufactured in the immediate vicinity of the necropolis. The various gold ornaments from the tombs have a close stylistic affinity with one another, so that it can be presumed with some degree of probability that they were made nearby.

The necropolis at Messambria dates back to the 3rd century B.C. The grave finds are today in the Historical Museum, Bourgas. Here is a typical inventory of one of the female burials: in addition to the obligatory jar there were 4 other clay vessels, 1 bronze mirror, 3 gold finger-rings (including a spiral ring in the form of a snake—see plate **40**), 1 pair of gold earrings (plate **35**), 2 gold necklaces, 1 silver fibula, 1 bronze fibula, 1 bronze bangle, 4 glass pearls, 1 clay pearl, 2 clay amulets.

1.14.1   Earrings of twisted gold wire with the thicker end in the form of a maenad's head
Dm 3 cm; Inv. Nos. 369, 370
Plate **35**

1.14.2   Earrings of gold wire with the thicker end fashioned as a Pegasus *protome* and pendants in the form of amphorae
Dm of the rings 2.7 cm, L of the pendants 3 cm; Inv. Nos. 1332, 1333
Plate **34**

1.14.3   Spiral gold finger-ring in the form of a snake
L 4 cm; Inv. No. 368
Plate **40**

1.14.4   Spiral gold ring in the form of a dragon, beset with amethysts
L 6.1 cm, Dm 2.1 cm; Inv. No. 1336
Plate **39**

1.15   Near Bryastovets, Bourgas district, a barrow from the 1st century A.D. was investigated. Beneath the earth-mound was a cist made of stone slabs. It contained the cremated remains of a man along with the following objects: 1 bronze ceremonial helmet decorated with reliefs depicting several Roman gods, 5 bronze vessels, 2 iron swords and 1 iron spearhead.

Bronze ceremonial helmet
H 19.7 cm, Dm 21 cm
Archaeological Museum, Sofia; Inv. No. 6176
Plate **53**

1.16   The necropolis of the Roman town of Trimontium (Thracian Pulpudeva, Greek Philippopolis, today Plovdiv) lay on a road which led eastwards out of the town. Beneath a barrow a burial chamber made of large stone slabs and bricks in the form of a sarcophagus was found which contained the cremated remains of a man. All the accompanying grave goods had clearly discernible burn marks. Outside the grave but still beneath the earth-mound a hearth was uncovered and near it burnt animal bones and parts of metal bridle trappings together with some iron nails which had been deformed by the fire. The following grave goods lay all of a heap in the grave chest: 1 gold finger-ring with gem, leaves of a wreath of gold foil, 1 helmet-mask of iron and silver, 2 silver goblets decorated with reliefs, 1 silver ladle, 4 bronze bowls, 2 bronze amphorae, 2 bronze jars, 1 bronze candlestick, 1 glass vessel, 1 iron vessel, 4 iron lance-tips, several carved bone handles, remains of leather straps and fragments of a number of metal objects which had been destroyed by the effects of the fire. All the objects from this tomb, which with reference to the helmet-mask has been dated to the first half of the 1st century A.D., are today in the Archaeological Museum, Plovdiv.

Helmet-mask. Calotte of iron, face and laurel wreath of silver
H 30 cm, W 16.5 cm; Inv. No. 19
Plate **54**

1.17   The surroundings of Stara Zagora are rich in archaeological finds. Near Chatalka, Stara Zagora district, a Roman villa complete with living apartments, slave quarters, stables and workshops was uncovered. In the environs of the villa there are seven grave mounds of which two have been investigated. Beneath one of them were found the cremated remains of a woman who had been lavishly provided with gold jewelry. Beneath the second mound two male graves—also cremations—were discovered of which one contained few grave goods. The other tomb was constructed at the end of the 1st century A.D.; it contained the following items which are today housed in the Historical Museum, Stara Zagora: 1 marble urn with a lid glued on with a lime-based mortar around which lay a wreath of gold oak and laurel leaves; 1 complete set of battle armor consisting of a breastplate, greaves, helmet, wooden or leather shield of which only a few metal fittings remain, iron spurs, 2 iron swords with gilt hilts, 50 iron arrowheads and 6 iron spearheads. In addition there were several gold and bronze fittings, 1 bronze scraper (strigilis), 7 bronze vessels, 1 bronze lamp, 1 bronze lantern, 1 bronze candelabra, 1 iron vessel and 1 hand-molded clay vessel.

> Ceremonial helmet-mask. Calotte of iron, face of silver-coated bronze
> H 23 cm; Inv. No. 2C 1116
> Plate **55**

1.18 During earthworks in preparation for the construction of a railway line near Shishkovtsi, Kyustendil district, the remains of two four-wheeled wooden chariots with a total of four horse skeletons were found at the edge of a tumulus which had been largely levelled out. For purposes of decoration and stabilization the chariots had been furnished with numerous metal parts and fittings. The wooden parts had rotted away, but the position of the metal parts made it possible to reconstruct the original appearance of these Thracian chariots from Roman times. To date a total of 50 such chariots have been traced on Thracian territory.

The finds of Shishkovtsi have been dated to the 2nd/3rd century A.D.; they are today in the Archaeological Museum, Sofia.

> Bronze fitting for a wooden chariot, decorated with a parcel-gilt silver bust of Heracles
> Dm 12.2 cm, H 22 cm; Inv. No. 7992
> Plate **49**

2. Chance discoveries of treasure

2.1 Near Pobit Kamuk, Razgrad district, a total of 7 stone molds for the production of bronze objects were found which date back to the late Bronze Age (c. 1500–1200 B.C.). They had been buried in the ground as treasure.

> Mold for the handle of a bronze scepter
> L 17 cm, W 25 cm
> Archaeological Museum, Sofia; Inv. No. 5086
> Plate **48**

2.2 Set of gold ritual vessels from Vulchitrun, Pleven district. The 13 items of this hoard are today in the Archaeological Museum, Sofia.

2.2.1 Two-handled vessel
H 22.4 cm; Inv. No. 3192

2.2.2 *Kyathos*
H 18.3 cm, Ldm 16.2 cm; Inv. No. 3193

2.2.3 Three *kyathoi*
H 8.2; 8.9; 8.9 cm, Ldm 4.5; 4.8; 4.9 cm; Inv. Nos. 3194, 3195, 3204

2.2.4 Two cymbals decorated with thin strips of silver
Dm 36 and 37 cm, H 12.6 cm; Inv. Nos. 3196, 3197

2.2.5 Five cymbals
Dm 21.5 and 21.6 cm, H 11.5 and 11.6 cm; Inv. Nos. 3198, 3199, 3200, 3201, 3202

2.2.6 Triple vessel
H 5.3 cm, W 23.9 cm; Inv. No. 3203
Plates **7–10**

2.3 During construction work in Kasichene, a suburb of Sofia, three vessels made of different materials were found which formed part of a treasure hoard which was buried between the 10th and 7th centuries B.C. Today they are in the Historical Museum, Sofia. The treasure also includes a gold *phiale*, a copper pot and a clay bowl.

> *Phiale* of stamped gold foil
> Ldm 24 cm, H 14.5 cm; Inv. No. 3014
> Plate **14**

2.4 During the ploughing of a field in the region of Daskal Atanasovo, Stara Zagora district, three similar gold *phialai* came to light. Only broken fragments remained of two of the *phialai*, but the third was still completely intact. They have been dated to the 5th century B.C.

> Gold *phiale* with embossed lotus blossom ornament
> H 3 cm, Dm 14.5 cm
> Historical Museum, Stara Zagora;
> Inv. No. 2C 31131
> Plate **13**

2.5   A treasure found near Radyuvene, Lovech district, contained 1 silver *aryballos*, 8 silver *phialai* and 2 decorative horse bridle plates. The objects were buried in the 5th/4th century B.C.; today they are in the Archaeological Museum, Sofia.

> Two silver plaques in the form of a lion's forequarters
> L 4 cm; Inv. Nos. 5201, 5202
> Plate **75**

2.6   In a hill cemetery near Borovo, Rousse district, several silver vessels from the first half of the 4th century B.C. were found. However, they were not grave goods but a hoard of buried treasure. The five vessels are today housed in the Historical Museum, Rousse.

2.6.1   *Rhyton* with horse *protome*
H 20.2 cm; Inv. No. II-357

2.6.2   *Rhyton* with sphinx *protome*
H 20.2 cm; Inv. No. II-358

2.6.3   *Rhyton* with bull *protome*
H 16.5 cm; Inv. No. II-359

2.6.4   Two-handled dish *(podanypter)*
Dm 29 cm; Inv. No. II-360

2.6.5   Handle-less *rhyton* in the form of a jar
H 18.2 cm; Inv. No. II-361
Plates **99−105**; **114**

2.7   In 1964 a hoard of treasure came to light by chance near the village of Vladinya, Lovech district. It had been buried around the middle of the 4th century B.C. in the ground and consisted of the following items which are today in the Archaeological Museum, Sofia: 1 silver *phiale*, 2 silver fibulae, 1 solid silver bangle and 36 fluted gold pearls from a necklace.

> Silver *phiale*
> Dm 10.5 cm, H 3.5 cm; Inv. No. 8150
> Plate **17**

2.8   Near Loukovit, Lovech district, a hoard was recovered which was probably buried towards the end of the 4th century B.C. at a time when armed conflict with the Macedonians had made life in Thrace insecure. The hoard comprises 5 silver goblets, 3 silver jars, 5 silver *phialai* and 3 sets of horse bridle trappings of which two depict largely animal motifs while the third is mainly decorated with plant ornaments. In addition there were some 200 silver plaques adorned with schematic representations of human faces.

The individual elements of the treasure in its present form were made and collected at various times between the 5th and late 4th centuries B.C. Today they are in the Archaeological Museum, Sofia.

2.8.1   Parcel-gilt silver *phiale* with reliefs of 8 female heads between palmette ornaments
H 7 cm, Dm 8.6 cm; Inv. No. 8226
Plate **12**

2.8.2   Parcel-gilt silver brow-piece
L 10 cm; Inv. No. 8212
Plate **78**

2.8.3   Two silver plaques
L 10.3 cm; Inv. Nos. 8197, 8198
Plate **76**

2.8.4   Four silver plaques in the form of a four-vaned swastika with griffin head terminals
L 10.3 cm, W 9.8 cm; Inv. Nos. 8193, 8196
Plate **82**

2.8.5   Two parcel-gilt silver plaques consisting of scroll ornaments and rosettes
L 8.7 cm, W 4.9 cm; Inv. Nos. 8204, 8205
Plate **83**

2.8.6   Two parcel-gilt silver plaques with irregular outlines
L 7.5 and 6.6 cm; Inv. Nos. 8213, 8214
Plate **84**

2.9   Near Letnitsa, Lovech district, a set of 22 metal plaques, 1 horse bridle frontlet and 1 snaffle were found inside a bronze vessel. The find, which dates from the second half of the 4th century B.C., is today in the Historical Museum, Lovech.

The plaques are made of silver foil and are partly gilt; they are square or rectangular and are between 4.2 and 7 cm long; 4 plaques in the form of squatting eagles (plate **78**) are only 2.8 cm long.

> Inv. Nos. 580−592, 594, 604−606
> Plates **79−81**, **85−98**, **71**

2.10   In 1949 in a loam-pit near Panagyurishte, Plovdiv district, a set of drinking vessels from the late 4th or early 3rd century B.C. was found. It consists of 9 gold vessels and is today in the Archaeological Museum, Plovdiv.

2.10.1   *Rhyton* with he-goat *protome*
H 14 cm; Inv. No. 3196

2.10.2   *Rhyton* in the form of a stag's head
H 13.5 cm; Inv. No. 3197

2.10.3 *Rhyton* in the form of a stag's head
H 12.5 cm; Inv.No. 3198

2.10.4 *Rhyton* in the form of a ram's head
H 12.5 cm; Inv.No. 3199

2.10.5 *Rhyton* in the form of a woman's head
H 14 cm; Inv.No. 3200

2.10.6 *Rhyton* in the form of a woman's head
H 22.5 cm; Inv.No. 3201

2.10.7 *Rhyton* in the form of a woman's head
H 20.5 cm; Inv.No. 3202

2.10.8 *Rhyton* in the form of an amphora
H 28 cm; Inv.No. 3203

2.10.9 *Phiale*
Dm 25 cm; Inv.No. 3204
Plates **106–113**

2.11 In 1918 on the outskirts of the village of Galiche, Smolyan district, 14 round, parcel-gilt silver plaques were found which had been swilled out of the ground by the action of water. Most of the *phalerae*, which were made in the 2nd/1st century B.C., are decorated with rosettes, but two carry figurative designs. All the objects are today in the Archaeological Museum, Sofia.

Two parcel-gilt silver *phalerae*
2.11.1 Dm 15.8 cm; Inv.No. 5877
It depicts a horseman facing to the left against a dotted background.

2.11.2 Dm 18.3 cm; Inv.No. 5876
This *phalera* shows a bust of the Great Mother-Goddess flanked by two birds.
Plate **32**

2.12 In 1972 a hoard of silver treasure was found near the village of Yakimovo, Mihailovgrad district, which is today housed in the Town Museum, Mihailovgrad. The find includes 4 silver bowls, 1 silver *kantharos*, 2 silver handles from vessels which are now lost, 2 bronze vessels, 2 silver *phalerae*, 2 silver bangles, 1 silver plaque and 1 bronze finger-ring. The items were buried in the 1st century B.C.

Silver bowl with gilt relief depicting a horseman
H 10.3 cm, Dm 16 cm; Inv.No. 46
Plate **20**

2.13 Near Golyama Brestnitsa, Lovech district, a set of silver ritual vessels were found which consisted of 1 cylindrical bowl and 5 small, one-handled casseroles. The bowl bears a Greek inscription on its upper edge: Presented to the God-Hero Pyrumerula by the Beneficiary (= member of the Roman army) Flavios Mestrianos. The same inscription appears on the upper side of the handle of one of the casserole dishes; on the handle of another plant ornaments are depicted; the handles of the remaining three casseroles are devoid of decoration.

2.13.1 Cylindrical silver bowl
Dm 22 cm, H 9 cm
Historical Museum, Pleven; Inv.No. 113

2.13.2 Five silver casseroles
Dm 7.4–9.5 cm, H 4–6 cm
Historical Museum, Pleven; Inv.Nos. 113-1 to 113-5
Plate **18**

2.14 In 1909 near the village of Nikolayevo, Pleven district, a hoard of treasure was found quite by chance. It consists of 6 dissimilar gold chains—some with pendants—, 1 pair of gold earrings with pendants, 1 lone gold earring, 1 gold torque, 6 gold bangles, 5 gold finger-rings with sardonyx inlays, 1 broad, openwork gold finger-ring with a Latin inscription dedicated to the hero Heracles, 1 silver saltcellar in the form of a girl with a dog on her lap, 1 silver *phiale*, 3 silver bangles, 1 silver finger-ring with a gemstone and 1 Roman bronze fibula. In addition to these items of jewelry the hoard also included 933 Roman silver coins, most of which were minted during the first half of the 3rd century A.D. The objects were buried in the ground in the year 248/249 at a time when the province of Moesia, to which the treasure belonged, was the victim of a large-scale invasion by the Goths. All the objects are today in the Archaeological Museum, Sofia.

2.14.1 Gold necklace
L 46.6 cm; Inv.No. 4774
It has a pendant in the form of a gold coin showing the Roman emperor Caracalla (211–217) framed by 8 precious stones.

2.14.2 Gold necklace with a green gemstone inset as pendant
L 41 cm; Inv.No. 4776

2.14.3 Bangle of plaited gold wire with hinged clasp
Dm 10 cm; Inv.No. 4783

2.14.4 Openwork gold bangle with spiral terminals
Dm 5 cm; Inv. No. 4784

2.14.5 Two gold bangles, hollow, with hinges
Dm 7.5 cm; Inv. Nos. 4784, 4785

2.14.6 Four gold finger-rings with sardonyx inlays
Dm 2.7–2.9 cm; Inv. Nos. 4792, 4793, 4794, 4796
Plate **45**

3. One-off individual finds

3.1 Three clay vessels from the late Stone or Chalcolithic Age

3.1.1 Vessel from a Neolithic settlement near Gradeshnitsa, Vratsa district
H 25.5 cm, W 19 cm
Historical Museum, Vratsa; Inv. No. A-2022
Neolithic, end of the 6th millennium B.C. High up on the neck is a stylized portrayal of a human face; the neck and wall are painted with geometric patterns.

3.1.2 Vessel from the hill settlement at Karanovo, Sliven district
H 18.5 cm
Archaeological Museum, Sofia; Inv. No. 3406
Neolithic, c. 4000 B.C.; surface of the vessel is adorned with plastic nodules, painted brown; handle in the form of a stylized animal.

3.1.3 Bowl from the hill settlement of Karanovo, Sliven district
H 16 cm
Archaeological Museum, Sofia; Inv. No. 4032
Late Chalcolithic Age, c. 3000 B.C. Black decoration and white incrusted pattern etched on a red background.
Plate **2**

3.2 Weapons from the late Bronze Age (c. 1500–1200 B.C.)

3.2.1 Bronze sword from the vicinity of the village of Dr. Yosifovo, Mihailovgrad district; Mycenaean type
L 45 cm
Archaeological Museum, Sofia; Inv. No. 3960

3.2.2 Bronze sword from Baikal, Pleven district
L 63.5 cm
Archaeological Museum, Sofia; Inv. No. 20
Its form bears an affinity to Bronze Age swords found to the north of the Thracian areas.

3.2.3 Bronze sword from Oryahovo, Varna district
L 63 cm
Archaeological Museum, Sofia; Inv. No. 3020
Its form resembles contemporary swords found to the north of the Thracian areas.

3.2.4 Bronze lance-tip from Sarantsi, Sofia district
L 19.2 cm, Dm of the shaft-hole 2.8 cm
Archaeological Museum, Sofia; Inv. No. 2755
Plate **66**

3.3 Gold decorative plate for a dagger sheath, found near Belogradets, Varna district, 8th/7th century B.C.
L 20.1 cm
Archaeological Museum, Sofia; Inv. No. 2865
Plate **46**

3.4 Bronze belt clasp and fitting from the same belt from the region of Vidin, 8th/7th century B.C.
L 9 and 5.1 cm
Archaeological Museum, Sofia; Inv. Nos. 124, 125
Plate **62**

3.5 Bronze helmet, found in Chelopechene near Sofia, end of the 6th century B.C.
H 20.9 cm
National War Museum, Sofia; Inv. No. 547/63
Plate **50**

3.6 Bronze matrix with two animal friezes for the decoration of metal goblets, found near Gurchinovo, Shoumen district, c. 5th century B.C.
L 34.5 cm, L of the design 29.5 cm, W 10.5–12 cm
Historical Museum, Shoumen; Inv. No. 23
Plate **11**

3.7 Two bangles of gold wire, found near Skrebatno, Blagoyevgrad district, 5th century B.C.
Dm 8.4 and 10 cm
Archaeological Museum, Sofia; Inv. Nos. 3167, 3168
Plate **64**

3.8 Bronze helmet
Place of discovery unknown, second half of the 5th century B.C.
H 21 cm
Archaeological Museum, Sofia; Inv. No. 4013
Plate **52**

3.9 Gold torque found near Cibur Varosh, Mihailovgrad district, 4th century B.C.
> Dm 14.5 cm
> Archaeological Museum, Sofia; Inv.No.3242
> Plate **31**

3.10 Gold earring from Boyana near Sofia, end of the 4th century B.C.
> L 10.1 cm
> Archaeological Museum, Sofia; Inv.No.2887
> Plate **30**

3.11 Thracian coins

3.11.1 Seuthes III (324–311 B.C.)
> Bronze, Dm 2.2 cm
> Archaeological Museum, Plovdiv; Inv.No.6435
> Obverse: the king's head facing right
> Reverse: horseman facing right

3.11.2 Kotys I (383–359 B.C.)
> Bronze, Dm 2.1 cm
> Archaeological Museum, Sofia; Inv.No.121
> Obverse: man's head facing left
> Reverse: two-handled vessel

3.11.3 Sparadokos (c. 424 B.C.)
> Silver, Dm 1.5 cm
> Archaeological Museum, Sofia; Inv.No.7219
> Obverse: cantering horse facing left
> Reverse: eagle with spread wings

3.11.4 Teres II (348 B.C.)
> Bronze, Dm 2.1 cm
> Archaeological Museum, Sofia; Inv.No.3187
> Obverse: double-headed axe
> Reverse: vine with grapes

3.11.5 Amadokos (359–351 B.C.)
> Bronze, Dm 2.1 cm
> Archaeological Museum, Sofia; Inv.No.8761
> Obverse: double-headed axe
> Reverse: grapevine
> Plate **4**

3.12 Two gold finger-rings

3.12.1 Finger-ring from Glozhene, Lovech district, 4th century B.C.
> Dm 2.8 cm
> Archaeological Museum, Sofia; Inv.No.7955

3.12.2 Finger-ring, place of discovery unknown, 4th century B.C.
> Dm 2.6 cm
> Archaeological Museum, Sofia; Inv.No.8398
> Plate **38**

3.13 Belt fitting, silver gilt, found near Lovets, Stara Zagora district, 5th/4th century B.C.
> L 31 cm
> Archaeological Museum, Sofia; Inv.No.6617
> Plate **63**

3.14 Bronze helmet in the form of a Phrygian cap, found near Gurmen, Blagoyevgrad district
> H 26 cm, Dm 24 cm
> Archaeological Museum, Sofia; Inv.No. 8246
> Plate **67**

3.15 Two bronze statuettes of the Thracian Horseman

3.15.1 Horseman figure from Drumohar, Kyustendil district
> H 7.5 cm
> Archaeological Museum, Sofia; Inv.No.7046
> The figure of the horse was found in Chavka, Kurdjali district
> H 7.8 cm
> Archaeological Museum, Sofia; Inv.No.6231

3.15.2 Horseman figure found in the ancient township of Deultum near Bourgas
> H 9 cm, L 7 cm
> Archaeological Museum, Sofia; Inv.Nos.5965, 5966
> Plate **61**

3.16 Votive relief for the Thracian Horseman, found near Kaspichan, Shoumen district; marble, dating from Roman times
> H 30 cm, W 25 cm
> Archaeological Museum, Sofia; Inv.No.1322
> Plate **60**

Glossary

Achaeans: Tribe which settled on the Greek mainland in the early part of the 2nd millennium B.C.; according to legend, the enemies and ultimately the conquerors of Troy.

Achaemenids: Ruling Persian dynasty from the 6th to the 4th centuries B.C. whose name derives from the mythical king Hakhamanish (Greek: Achaimenes).

Agamemnon: King of Mycenae, brother of Menelaus and leader of the Achaeans in the war against Troy.

Alexander the Great: Alexander III, king of Macedon (356–323 B.C.), founder of an enormous world empire which, however, disintegrated after his death.

Amazons: According to Greek legend, a race of men-hating and bellicose women living in Asia Minor.

anthropomorphous: Having the form of a human being.

Aphrodite: Greek goddess of love.

Apollo: Greek god of light whom the Thracians also greatly revered in connection with sun worship.

apotropaic: Warding off evil.

appliqué: Small metal plaque used for the decoration of clothing, armor, horse bridles or wooden chariots; made of cast metal and sometimes bearing embossed reliefs.

Ariadne: Daughter of the Cretan king Minos who helped the Athenian Theseus in his struggle with the Minotaur by giving him a thread to enable him to find his way back out of the labyrinth. She fled with Theseus but was deserted by him on the island of Naxos where Dionysus found her and made her his wife.

autochthonous: Denoting the original inhabitants of a place, as opposed to later immigrants.

Bronze Age: Era in which bronze—an alloy of copper and tin— was overwhelmingly used in the manufacture of tools, ornaments and weapons; on the Balkan peninsula the term roughly covers the 3rd and 2nd millennia B.C. It presupposes the knowledge and application of technologies for the extraction and processing of metals.

Burebista: Dacian king (86–44 B.C.) who succeeded in forging the separate Dacian tribes into a powerful union. In 48 B.C. he supported Pompey in the latter's struggle against Caesar; he was assassinated in 44 B.C.

Caesar: Roman statesman and general (100–44 B.C.). In his struggle against Pompey the Dacians, under Burebista, were also ranged against him. After defeating Pompey he planned a retaliatory campaign against the Dacians, but did not live long enough to realize it.

Celts: See Galatians.

cenotaph: Tomb without a burial; monument, e.g. for a general who died far from home.

centaur: Fabulous creature in Greek mythology with the legs and body of a horse and the shoulders and arms of a man.

Chalcolithic Age: Era of Stone and Copper. On the Balkan peninsula it denotes the late 4th millennium B.C., a period when, in addition to stone, naturally occurring metals such as copper and gold were used for making implements.

chlamys: Article of Greek clothing consisting of a short woollen cloak fastened at one shoulder by a clasp; worn especially by men when travelling and by soldiers.

client relationship: Originally a bilateral agreement of mutual support. In the wake of their expansion the Romans made use of this form of treaty in order to subjugate nations which they had not yet overthrown while formally granting them autonomy and protection.

colonization: Movement emanating from the Greek *poleis* between the 8th and 6th centuries B.C. in the course of which Greek towns (colonies) were founded on the coasts of the Mediterranean and the Black Sea.

Dacia: Roman province north of the Danube; established after Emperor Trajan's victory over the Dacians in A.D. 106; *c.* 273 A.D. the Romans had to cede the province.

Dacians: Thracian tribe, or people closely related to the Thracians, living north of the Danube in what is today Romania.

Dardanae: Thracian tribe living partly on the Balkan peninsula and partly along the Asia Minor seaboard in the environs of Troy.

Darius I: Persian king (522–486 B.C.) from a collateral line of the Achaemenids.

Decebalus: Last king of the Dacians (A.D. 85–106); he fought two wars against the Roman emperor Trajan (in A.D. 101/102 and 105/106); committed suicide at the end of the second war after the Romans had captured the Dacian capital Sarmizegetusa.

Delian League: Modern term denoting a maritime alliance of numerous Greek coastal towns and islands led by Athens which emerged in the first half of the 5th century B.C. from the unification of the Greeks in face of the Persian threat; for a time the Odrysian kingdom also belonged to it.

diadochoi: Officers of Alexander the Great who, after his death in 323 B.C., divided up his empire into smaller domains.

Dionysus: Greek god of wine, according to one version of the legend born in Thrace.

dolmen: Simple tomb of large, natural or barely worked slabs of stone, widespread in south-eastern Thrace during the early Iron Age (8th to 6th centuries B.C.).

Eneolithic Age: See Chalcolithic Age.

ethnogenesis: Formation process of a nation. The ethnogenesis of the Thracians was accomplished during the Bronze Age and involved the fusion of the indigenous population with various groups of immigrants; by around the end of the 2nd millennium B.C. the process was complete.

fluting: Vertical grooves on Greek columns; on metal vessels they may also run horizontally or radially and be worked up into convex or concave reliefs.

Galatians: Indo-European people in western Europe which migrated eastwards in the first half of the 3rd century B.C., occupied the Thracian Balkan peninsula for a time and also threatened Greece and Asia Minor.

Getae: Thracian tribe living to the north and south of the Danube delta in what is now south-eastern Romania; they are often equated with the Dacians.

gladiators: Professional fighters or sometimes specially trained slaves in the Roman empire who had to engage in exhibition fights with fixed rules which often had a fatal outcome.

Heracles: Greek hero, the son of Zeus and the mortal Alcmene; specially renowned for the 12 labors which he had to perform for Eurystheus in order to gain admission to Olympus; these included killing the Nemean lion and capturing the Cerynean hind.

Herodotus: Greek historian who lived from 484 to 425 B.C.; his travels also took him to Thrace, which he then described in his histories.

hippocampus: Mythical sea horse ridden by maritime deities.

Homer: Greek epic poet who lived in the 8th century B.C. In his *Iliad* he celebrated the legendary ten-year war of the Achaeans against Ilium (= Troy) and in the *Odyssey* the ten years of adventures which befell the Greek hero Odysseus after the end of the Trojan War.

hydria: Three-handled Greek vessel for carrying water.

Iron Age: Era which on the Balkan peninsula set in at the turn of the 2nd and 1st millennia B.C. and which was characterized by the fact that iron was the main metal used for making tools and weapons.

kantharos: Two-handled Greek drinking vessel which was the attribute of the wine-god Dionysus and his followers.

krater: Two-handled vessel with wide lip used for mixing wine and water.

kyathos: One-handled cup-like vessel.

labyrinth: In Greek mythology a mighty maze of winding passages which Daedalus built in Knossos for the Cretan king Minos in which the Minotaur was kept hidden.

Lysimachus: *c.* 355–281 B.C., one of Alexander the Great's officers who, on the latter's death, took charge of Thrace and parts of Asia Minor; king of Thrace from 305 B.C. onwards.

Macedonians: Neighboring tribe living to the south-west of the Thracians.

maenads: Female companions of the wine-god Dionysus.

Menelaus: Mycenaean prince in Sparta married to Helen, whose abduction by the Trojan prince Paris allegedly triggered off the Trojan War.

Minotaur: Legendary monster, offspring of Pasiphaë, the wife of the Cretan king Minos, and a sacred bull. The Minotaur demanded a tribute of young girls and boys from the Athenians until Theseus killed it.

Moesia: Roman border province on the Danube (situated in what is now Hungary, Yugoslavia and northern Bulgaria) established in A.D. 15. Ceded by the Romans in A.D. 600 after which Avars and Slavs settled in the area.

Moesians: Thracian tribe located south of the Danube in what is today northern Bulgaria.

Mycenae: Important state and civilization on the Greek mainland during the late Bronze Age (second half of the 2nd millennium B.C.).

necropolis: Large urban cemetery.

Neolithic Age: Last period of the Stone Age, covering the 6th to 4th millennia B.C. on the Balkan peninsula, when stone —particularly flint—was used for the manufacture of tools. The Neolithic Age marked the start of systematically organized farming and of the production of clay vessels.

Nereid: One of the fifty daughters of the sea-god Nereus.

Nereus: Greek sea-god.

Odrysae: Thracian tribe living to the south of the Balkan mountains; in the 5th century B.C. they founded a kingdom which covered much of the south-eastern part of the Balkan peninsula.

omphalos: Greek word for navel; sacred stone in Delphi which was believed to mark the center of the earth, whence it then came to denote the raised central boss inside offering bowls *(phialai)*.

pectoral: Breastplate; also a decorative metal plaque sewed or fixed by a fibula onto clothing across the chest.

Pegasus: Winged horse in Greek mythology born just as Perseus cut off the head of the Gorgon.

phalera: Round, ornamental metal disk attached to leather armor or horse bridle straps.

phiale: Greek term for a shallow offering bowl with a raised central boss *(omphalos)*.

Philip II: King of Macedon (382–336 B.C.) who extended Macedonian rule over Greece and Thrace; father of Alexander the Great.

polis: Greek city-state which formed the basis for the development of democracy in antiquity.

Pompey: Roman statesman and general (106–48 B.C.); was supported by the Dacians in his struggle with Caesar.

Proto-Bulgarians: Tribe of horsemen led by Asparukh which settled in the Balkan peninsula in the middle of the 7th century A.D. and played a fundamental role in the founding of the first Bulgarian kingdom in 681.

protome: Design, as used for example on drinking vessels *(rhyta)*, in the form of the forequarters of an animal or imaginary creature.

rhyton: Funnel-shaped drinking vessel which may be wholly or partly given a figurative design.

satrap: Provincial governor appointed by the Persian king.

satyr: Youthful male companion of Dionysus, often depicted with pointed animal ears and a tail.

Scythians: North-eastern neighbors of the Thracians.

Silenus: According to Greek legend he was the tutor of Dionysus and later became one of his attendants; in time the term came to designate the god's older male companions.

situla: Greek vessel resembling a pail.

Slavs: Indo-European people which settled in the Balkan peninsula in the 6th to 7th centuries A.D. and which became one of the principal constituents of the Bulgarian nation.

Spartacus: Thracian who arrived in Italy as a slave and was trained as a gladiator in Capua; leader of the biggest slave revolt in antiquity (74–71 B.C.).

tell: Artificial hill formed by the deposits of several superimposed settlements.

Theseus: Prince and hero whose many exploits, according to Greek legend, included freeing his native city of Athens from the sway of the Cretan king Minos by the slaying of the Minotaur; later he became king of Athens.

Thucydides: Greek historian (*c.* 460–396 B.C.); leased gold mines in Thrace and lived there for 20 years.

toreutics: The cold-working of metals, e.g. by chasing, engraving, boring and embossing.

torque: Metal necklace, especially popular among the Celts, worn both as a badge of rank and as an ornament.

Triballi: Thracian tribe which settled an area to the south of the Danube corresponding to north-western Bulgaria.

Troy: Important Bronze Age metropolis on the western coast of Asia Minor; destroyed at the end of the 2nd millennium B.C.

umbo: Latin term for the raised central boss of an offering bowl; see *omphalos*.

Xenophon: Greek historian (*c.* 430–354 B.C.) who, at the head of a Greek mercenary army in 401 B.C., spent some time at the court of the Odrysian king.

zoomorphic: In the form of an animal.

SELECTED BIBLIOGRAPHY

In: *L'Europe à la fin de l'âge de la pierre. Actes du Symposium consacré aux problèmes du Néolithique européen.* Prague, 1961, pp. 45–100.

GEORGIEV, G. I. "Die Entwicklung der älteren prähistorischen Kulturen in Südbulgarien". In: *Studia balcanica 5* (1971), pp. 21–35.

GOČEVA, Z. and M. OPPERMANN *Corpus cultus equitis Thracii.* Vol. I. Leiden, 1979; Vol. II 1, 1981.

Goldschätze der Thraker. Thrakische Kunst und Kultur auf bulgarischem Boden. Exhibition Catalog. Berlin, 1978.

HÄNSEL, B. (editor) *Südosteuropa zwischen 1600 und 1000 v. Chr.* Berlin, 1982.

ANGELOV, D. *Die Entstehung des bulgarischen Volkes.* Berlin, 1980.

BERCIU, D. "Das thrako-getische Fürstengrab von Agighiol in Rumänien". In: *Berichte der Römisch-Germanischen Kommission 50* (1969), pp. 209–265.

BERCIU, D. *Contribution à l'étude de l'art thraco-gète.* Bucharest, 1974.

CANOVA, G. and L. GETOV *Kazanlik.* Sofia, 1965.

CASSON, S. *Macedonia, Thrace and Illyria.* Oxford, 1926.

Die Daker. Archäologie in Rumänien. Exhibition Catalog. Cologne, 1980.

DANOV, C. *Altthrakien.* Berlin, 1976.

DETSCHEW, D. *Die thrakischen Sprachreste.* Vienna, 1957.

DIMITROV, D. P. "Seuthopolis". In: *Antiquity 25*, N. 138 (1961), pp. 91–102.

DIMITROV, D. P. "Troia VII b2 und die thrakischen und mösischen Stämme auf dem Balkan". In: *Studia balcanica 5* (1971), pp. 63–78.

FETICH, N. *Der skythische Fund von Gartschinovo.* Budapest, 1935.

FILOV, B. "Denkmäler der thrakischen Kunst". In: *Izvestija na Bălgarskoto Archeologičesko družestvo 6* (1919), p. 5 sqq.

FILOV, B. *Die Grabhügel von Duvanlij.* Sofia, 1934.

FLORESCU, F. B. *Das Siegesdenkmal von Adamklisi—Tropaeum Traiani.* Bucharest-Bonn, 1965.

FOL, A. "Die Dorfgemeinde in Thrakien im 1. Jahrtausend v.u.Z.". In: *Jahrbuch für Wirtschaftsgeschichte 1969*, part 1, pp. 279–322.

FOL, A. *Političeska istorija na trakite ot kraja na II chiljadoletie do kraja na V v. pr. n. e.* Sofia, 1972.

FOL, A. *Trakija i Elada prez krizata ot IV v. pr. n. e.* Sofia, 1971.

GEORGIEV, G. I. "Kulturgruppen der Jungstein- und der Kupferzeit in der Ebene von Thrazien (Südbulgarien)".

IVANOV, D. "Der Silberschatz von Borovo". In: *Das Altertum 26* (1980), pp. 5–12.

KAZAROV, G. I. *Beiträge zur Kulturgeschichte der Thraker.* Sarajevo, 1916.

KAZAROV, G. I. *Die Denkmäler des Thrakischen Reitergottes in Bulgarien.* Budapest, 1938.

KOLEV, K. "Der thrakische Goldschatz von Panagjurište". In: *Das Altertum 26* (1980), pp. 204–215.

MIKOV, V. *Le tombeau antique près de Kasanlik.* Sofia, 1954.

MIKOV, V. *Le trésor d'or de Vălčitrăn, arr. de Pleven.* Sofia, 1958.

MIKOV, V. "La Bulgarie à l'âge du bronze". In: *Studia balcanica 5* (1971), pp. 51–61.

MILČEV, A. "Thrakische Siedlungen und Festungen in Bulgarien während des 1. Jahrtausends v.u.Z.". In: *Actes du IIe Congrès International de Thracologie.* Vol. 1. Bucharest, 1980, pp. 343–364.

OPPERMANN, M. "Zum Menschenbild der Thraker in vorrömischer Zeit". In: *Wissenschaftliche Zeitschrift der Martin-Luther-Universität Halle-Wittenberg. Gesellschafts- und sprachwissenschaftliche Reihe 25* (1976), no. 3, pp. 91–102.

OPPERMANN, M. "Zum Problem von Kunst und Gesellschaft in den römischen Provinzen Thracia und Moesia inferior". In: *Wissenschaftliche Zeitschrift der Martin-Luther-Universität Halle-Wittenberg. Gesellschafts- und sprachwissenschaftliche Reihe 30* (1981), no. 5, pp. 113–126.

SCHÖNERT-GEISS, E. "Zur Geschichte Thrakiens anhand von griechischen Münzbildern aus der römischen Kaiserzeit". In: *Klio 49* (1967), pp. 217–264.

TAČEVA-HITOVA, M. *Altthrakien und der europäische Südosten.* Sofia, 1976.

VELKOV, V. *Cities in Thrace and Dacia in late antiquity.* Amsterdam, 1977.

VENEDIKOV, I. *Der Goldschatz von Panagurischte.* Sofia, 1961.

VENEDIKOV, I. *Alte Schätze aus Bulgarien.* Sofia, 1965.

VENEDIKOV, I. and T. GERASIMOV *Thrakische Kunst.* Leipzig, 1975.

VENEDIKOV, I. *et al. Nessebre I.* Sofia, 1969.

VULPE, R. *L'âge du fer dans les régions thraces de la péninsule balcanique.* Paris, 1930.

VULPE, R. *Studia Thracologica.* Bucharest, 1976.

WIESNER, J. *Die Thraker.* Stuttgart, 1963.

Acknowledgments
Plates No. 3 and 7 were provided by FOREK, Sofia
(E. Enev/Popov).

Index